A Treatise On Painting

Leonardo da Vinci

Engraved by W.H. Worthington.

Published by J.B.Nichols & Son Parliament Street.

A

TREATISE

ON

PAINTING,

BY

LEONARDO DA VINCI:

FAITHFULLY TRANSLATED FROM THE ORIGINAL
ITALIAN,

AND DIGESTED UNDER PROPER HEADS,

By JOHN FRANCIS RIGAUD, Esq.

ACADEMICIAN OF THE ROYAL ACADEMY OF PAINTING AT LONDON,
AND ALSO OF THE ACADEMIA CLEMENTINA AT BOLOGNA,
AND THE ROYAL ACADEMY AT STOCKHOLM.

ILLUSTRATED WITH TWENTY-THREE COPPER-PLATES,
AND OTHER FIGURES.

TO WHICH IS PREFIXED A LIFE OF THE AUTHOR,
WITH A CRITICAL ACCOUNT OF HIS WORKS,

By JOHN WILLIAM BROWN, Esq.

LONDON:
J. B. NICHOLS AND SON, 25, PARLIAMENT STREET.
SOLD ALSO BY
W. PICKERING, CHANCERY LANE; J. WEALE, HIGH HOLBORN;
AND J. WILLIAMS, CHARLES STREET, SOHO.

1835.

Ars est habitus quidam faciendi vera cum ratione.
Aristot. Ethic. Lib. 6.

CONTENTS.

DIRECTIONS TO THE BINDER.

PREFACE.

Since the former edition of this work was published, the able Translator has paid the debt of nature.*

Mr. Rigaud being himself a painter, and highly appreciating the merits of Leonardo da Vinci, felt that he should derive pleasure from exhibiting his well-known Treatise on Painting to the British public with superior advantage. He, therefore, not only gave a new translation, but formed a better arrangement of the materials. The merits of Mr. Rigaud's Translation having been duly appreciated by the public, and the work having been long out of print, another edition, in a neater and more condensed form, is now produced, which, the Publishers presume, may prove a desirable acquisition to students and amateurs.

The principal novelty, however, of this edition is the new Life of the Author, by the late J. W. Brown, Esq., which was first published, in a separate volume, in 1828. A long residence in Italy, an intimate acquaintance with its language

* See a memoir of Mr. Rigaud, p. c.

A 3

and literature, together with a constant opportunity of studying the most finished specimens of Art, induced that gentleman to undertake the biography of LEONARDO DA VINCI, who so largely contributed to form a new æra in the History of the Fine Arts. This distinguished Italian *i*s not so well known in England as he deserves.

Among the various biographical sketches of this celebrated character, that written by Giorgio Vasari is perhaps the most authentic, as he had the advantage of contemporaneous information. But this also is rather an account of his works than of himself, containing little more than what is generally known, and forming only one article in Vasari's Lives of celebrated Painters.

To most of the editions which have been published of Da Vinci's writings a short biographical notice is prefixed, but they are chiefly copied verbatim from Vasari.

The Signor Carlo Ammoretti, librarian of the Ambrosian Library at Milan, has prefixed the best and most ample account of Leonardo da Vinci to the edition of his "Trattato della Pittura," published at Milan in 1804; which he has entitled " Memorie storiche su la Vita, gli Studj, e le Opere di Leonardo da Vinci."

In addition to many sources of information, Mr. Brown had the privilege of constant admittance not only to the private library of his Imperial and

Royal Highness the Grand Duke of Tuscany, but also to his most rare and valuable collection of Manuscripts in the Palazzo Pitti, where he was permitted to copy from the original documents and correspondence whatever he conceived useful to his subject.

In selecting from the mass of documents relative to the subject of the present work, Mr. Brown rejected whatever appeared unsupported by sufficient proof; and he has given such historical anecdotes of that period as were necessary to the subject, from their having materially influenced the private fortunes of Da Vinci.

Sept. 5, 1835.

PREFACE

Mr. RIGAUD'S TRANSLATION.

THE excellence of the following Treatise is so well known to all in any tolerable degree conversant with the Art of Painting, that it would be almost superfluous to say any thing respecting it, were it not that it here appears under the form of a new translation, of which some account may be expected.

Of the original Work, which is in reality a selection from the voluminous manuscript collections of the Author, both in folio and in quarto, of all such passages as related to Painting, no edition appeared in print till 1651, though its Author died so long before as the year 1519; and it is owing to the circumstance of a manuscript copy of these extracts in the original Italian, having fallen into the hands of Raphael du Fresne, that in the former of these years it was published at Paris in a thin folio volume in that language, accompanied with a set of cuts from the drawings of Nicolo

Poussin and Alberti; the former having designed the human figures, the latter the geometrical and other representations. This precaution was probably necessary, the sketches in the Author's own collections being so very slight as not to be fit for publication without further assistance. Poussin's drawings were mere outlines, and the shadows and back-grounds behind the figures were added by Errard, after the drawings had been made, and, as Poussin himself says, without his knowledge.

In the same year, and size, and printed at the same place, a translation of the original work into French was given to the world by Monsieur de Chambray (well known, under his family name of Freart, as the author of an excellent Parallel of ancient and modern Architecture, in French, which Mr. Evelyn translated into English). The style of this translation by Mons. de Chambray, being thought, some years after, too antiquated, some one was employed to revise and modernise it; and in 1716 a new edition of it, thus polished, came out, of which it may be truly said, as is in general the case on such occasions, that whatever the supposed advantage obtained in purity and refinement of language might be, it was more than counterbalanced by the want of the more valuable qualities of accuracy, and fidelity to the original, from which, by these variations, it became further removed.

The first translation of this Treatise into English,
appeared in the year 1721. It does not declare
by whom it was made; but though it professes to
have been done from the original Italian, it is
evident, upon a comparison, that more use was
made of the revised edition of the French translation. Indifferent, however, as it is, it had become
so scarce, and had risen to a price so extravagant,
that, to supply the demand, it was found necessary, in the year 1796, to reprint it as it stood,
with all its errors on its head, no opportunity then
offering of procuring a fresh translation.

This last impression, however, being also disposed of, and a new one again called for, the
present Translator was induced to step forward,
and undertake the office of fresh translating it, on
finding, by comparing the former versions both in
French and English with the original, many passages which he thought might at once be more
concisely and more faithfully rendered. His object, therefore, has been to attain these ends, and
as rules and precepts like the present allow but
little room for the decorations of style, he has
been more solicitous for fidelity, perspicuity, and
precision, than for smooth sentences, and well-
turned periods.

Nor was this the only advantage which it was
found the present opportunity would afford; for
the original work consisting in fact of a number

of entries made at different times, without any
regard to their subjects, or attention to method,
might rather in that state be considered as a chaos
of intelligence, than a well-digested treatise. It
has now, therefore, for the first time, been attempted to place each chapter under the 'proper
head or branch of the art to which it belongs
and by so doing, to bring together those which
(though related and nearly connected in substance)
stood, according to the original arrangement, at
such a distance from each other as to make it
troublesome to find them even by the assistance
of an index; and difficult, when found, to compare them together.

The consequence of this plan, it must be confessed, has been, that in a few instances the same
precept has been found in substance repeated;
but this is so far from being an objection, that it
evidently proves the precepts were not the hasty
opinions of the moment, but settled and fixed
principles in the mind of the Author, and that he
was consistent in the expression of his sentiments.
But if this mode of arrangement has in the present case disclosed what might have escaped observation, it has also been productive of more
material advantages; for, besides facilitating the
finding of any particular passage (an object in
itself of no small importance), it clearly shows the
work to be a much more complete system than

those best acquainted with it had before any idea
of, and that many of the references in it, apparently to other writings of the same Author, relate
in fact only to the present, the chapters referred
to having been found in it. These are now pointed
out in the notes, and where any obscurity has oc-
curred in the text, the reader will find some assistance at least attempted by the insertion of a note
to solve the difficulty.

No pains or expense have been spared in preparing the present work for the press. The cuts
have been re-engraved with more attention to
correctness in the drawing, than those which accompanied the two editions of the former English
translation possessed (even though they had been
fresh engraven for the impression of 1796); and
the diagrams are now inserted in their proper
places in the text, instead of being, as before, collected all together in two plates at the end.

J. F. RIGAUD.

1802.

THE LIFE

LEONARDO DA VINCI.

AMONG the many distinguished individuals who flourished in Italy during the early part of the sixteenth century, there is none more worthy of commemoration than Leonardo da Vinci, whether we consider his splendid and almost universal talents, or the excellence of his character. Through a long and active life his mind was zealously devoted to the revival of the arts, to which he contributed in a greater degree, perhaps, than any single individual of ancient or modern times. The arts of poetry, music, and especially painting, were embraced by him with an enthusiasm which awakened that of others, and gave a mighty impulse to the mental energies, not only of his contemporaries and countrymen, but of distant nations and posterity. Every incident in the life of such a man must be full of interest to the lovers of biography : the more so from the very remarkable fact, that in no language have those incidents been properly collected, though abundant and authentic sources of information exist on which such a work might be founded. To supply in some degree this deficiency, is the object of the following pages.

b

Leonardo da Vinci was born in the year 1452, at Vinci, in the Val d'Arno Inferiore, on the confines of the Pistoiese territory, not far from the Lake of Fucecchio. He was the natural son of Pietro da Vinci; and it is said that his mother was a servant in his father's family; but this must remain uncertain, from the length of time that has since elapsed, and the numerous reports that contradict each other, not only in what relates to his origin, but even to the year of his birth, in which there is a difference of no less than ten years. It is, however, certain, that he was entirely brought up in his father's family; a fact attested by an old and well authenticated register, found among the ancient archives of Florence by Signore Dei, who has written largely on the subject of Leonardo's genealogy. It is a matter of some regret, that, amidst all his learned and elaborate researches, that gentleman has not been able to procure any documents to prove that Da Vinci was subsequently declared legitimate, which from various circumstances appears to be extremely probable. If we may believe the register, and there is no better authority, Leonardo was seventeen years old when his father was forty; so that he must have been born when Pietro was a young man, and most likely before his marriage.

His father had three wives, Giovanna da Zenobi Amadori, Francesca di Ser Giuliano Lanfredini, and Lucrezia di Guglielmo Cortigiani; and a proof that Leonardo still formed a part of his family after his third marriage, is afforded by a passage in one of Belincionni's sonnets, addressed to Madonna Lucrezia da Vinci, which begins

"A Fiesole con Piero e Leonardo;"

and relates the pleasures he enjoyed at their villa near Florence. It is hardly probable that he would have received such unvarying attentions, had he been considered merely as a natural child. Moreover, we find from several documents in the " Codice Atlantico," that his family were at all times proud of his relationship, and his uncle Francesco da Vinci left him an equal share of his property with his other brothers and sisters.

Leonardo was gifted with one of the finest forms that can be imagined, in which strength and symmetry were beautifully combined ; his face was strongly expressive of his ardent mind, and of the frankness and energy of his character. He would, it may be presumed, have distinguished himself in the literary world while in his youth, had he not been as unsteady as he was enthusiastic in his various pursuits. He made such wonderful progress in arithmetic, that when a child he frequently proposed questions which his master himself was unable to resolve. He next attached himself to music as a science, and soon arrived at such perfection in playing on the lyre, which was his favourite instrument, as to compose extemporaneous accompaniments to his own poetical effusions. The following sonnet is one of the very few which are extant.

" Chi non può quel che vuol, quel che può voglia ;
Che quel che non si può folle è il volere.
Adunque saggio è l'uomo da tenere
Che da quel che non può suo voler toglia.
Pero che ogni diletto nostro e doglia
Stà in sì e no, saper voler potere,
Adunque quel sol può che è col dovere,
Ne trae la ragion fuor di sua soglia.

Ne sempre è da voler quel che l'uom pòte,
    Spesso par dolce quel che torna amaro,
    Piansi già quel che io volsi, poiche io l'hebbi.
Adunque tu, lettor di queste note,
    Se a te vuoi esser buono, e ad altri caro,
    Vogli sempre poter quel che tu debbi."

But, although an ardent admirer of the arts in general, painting appeared to be his favourite pursuit, to which he more particularly applied himself in all its different branches ; and in which he soon attained great excellence, as well as in the art of forming models and designs.

The praiseworthy exertions of Cimabue, Giotto, and Masaccio, had already begun to revive the art of painting in Italy, and particularly in Tuscany, where the arts were most certain to find protection and encouragement, from the powerful patronage of Lorenzo de' Medici, so justly styled " the Magnificent." His liberality had already acquired for his native Florence the honourable appellation of the " Modern Athens;" and his taste for literature and the fine arts considerably influenced the state of public opinion among his countrymen.

The Signore Pietro, perceiving that his son's abilities and inclinations might lead to future wealth and fame, determined to show the productions of his self-cultivated talents to Andrea Varocchio, one of the most celebrated painters, sculptors, and architects of that age.* Masser Andrea, surprised at the strong indi-

---

* Andrea del Varocchio, or Verrocchio, a Florentine painter, architect, and jeweller, died at Venice in 1488, where he was employed in forming the equestrian statue of Bartolomeo Coglioni in bronze. He was more celebrated as an architect and sculptor than as a painter.—See his life by Vasari.

cations of original talent and hope of future excellence,
which these early productions evinced, gladly consented to receive the young Leonardo into his
" studio," convinced that a pupil of so much merit
could not fail of increasing his master's celebrity ; but
he soon found that his scholar had very little need of
his instructions, and that he would ere long surpass
him in his own works.

It happened about this time that Messer Andrea
was employed to paint a picture of St. John baptizing
our Saviour ; and anxious to stimulate his young pupil
to greater exertion, he desired his assistance in this
composition.   Leonardo executed the part assigned
him with such extraordinary skill, that, as Vasari
relates, the angel painted by him greatly excelled all
the rest of Andrea's picture, which, he says, " was
the occasion of Messer Andrea's leaving off painting, enraged that a child should know more than
himself."

Having given this proof of wonderful abilities, he
employed himself in studying the different branches
of the art to which he now intended more particularly
to devote his attention.   But the natural inconstancy
of his disposition frequently impelled him to desert his
studio, and indulge in imaginary speculations.   His
time, however, was never unemployed ; and though
his occupations were always various, and sometimes
inconsistent, he nevertheless most assiduously cultivated whatever was calculated to adorn his mind or
increase his accomplishments.   He must also have
worked very diligently at his profession, as his father
could not have afforded him much money for his
amusements ; and he is known, if we may believe his

contemporaries, to have led rather a gay life. The delight of society wherever he went, and an extraordinary favourite with the fair sex, he became too fond of dress and parade; he maintained a numerous retinue of servants, a sumptuous equipage, and purchased the most spirited horses that could be procured. These extravagances were, however, extremely pardonable in a young man flushed with success and conscious of his superior acquirements, particularly as they could only be supported by the produce of his own industry, and must therefore have greatly tended to stimulate his exertions.

Like most people who are endowed with great natural talents, he undertook much more than he was able to accomplish; and we find him continually changing his occupations: at one time diligently employing himself in astronomical observations, to ascertain the motion of the heavenly bodies, at another intently pursuing the study of natural history and botany, yet with all his versatility of talent and inconstancy of disposition, never permitting himself to neglect his favourite pursuit. With the utmost perseverance he sought every possible means of improving himself in painting, from the time he left the studio of Andrea Varocchio, and became his own master.

The numerous works on scientific subjects that Leonardo has left to posterity, sufficiently prove how well he must have employed his youth, though very little is to be found in the writings of his contemporaries to give us any information of the occurrences of his every-day life. Both Vasari and Lomazzo relate that he invented various machines for lifting great weights, penetrating mountains, conducting water from

one place to another, and innumerable models for
watches, windmills, and presses. Two of the many
projects which he had in contemplation, some of which
were almost too wild for belief, deserve to be particularly noticed.   One of them was to lift up the Cathedral of San Lorenzo bodily, or rather *en masse,*
by means of immense levers, and in such a manner
that he pretended the edifice would not receive the
slightest injury.   The other, which was more feasible,
was to form the Arno into a canal as far as Pisa, and
which would have been extremely beneficial to the
commerce of Tuscany.

That Leonardo continued to reside at Florence, or
at least in its neighbourhood, is confirmed by the
story Vasari relates of the " Rotella del Fico," which
was a round piece of wood cut from the largest fig-tree
on his father's estate. The Signore Pietro was very
fond of field sports and country amusements; and one
of his " contadini" who was particularly useful to
him on these occasions, brought him a piece of wood,
requesting him to have something painted on it as an
ornament for his cottage.   Willing to gratify his
favourite, he desired his son to do as the man wished ;
and Leonardo determined to paint something that
should astonish his father by the great progress he
had made in his art.   This piece of wood must have
been roughly made and badly put together, as our
young artist was obliged to have it planed off and
the insterstices filled up with stucco, so as to leave a
surface sufficiently smooth for his purpose. He then
considered for some time what he should represent,
and at length determined on painting a monster that
should have the effect of Medusa's head on all be-

holders. For this purpose he collected every kind of reptile, vipers, adders, lizards, toads, serpents, and other poisonous or obnoxious animals, and formed a monster so wonderfully designed, that it appeared to flash fire from its eyes, and almost to infect the air with its breath. When he had succeeded to his wishes in this horrible composition, he called his father to try its effect upon him; who, not expecting what he was to see, started back with horror and affright, and was just going to run out of the room, when Leonardo stopped him by assuring him it was the work of his own hands, exclaiming, " that he was quite satisfied, as his picture had the effect he anticipated." The Signore Pietro was, of course, too much delighted with his son's performance to think of giving it to his " contadino," for whom he procured an ordinary painting, and sold Leonardo's to a merchant of Florence for one hundred ducats. This was a very large sum to give for a picture, when the value of money at the time is remembered; but it was soon after sold to the Duke of Milan for three times the original cost.

The life of a painter, however celebrated, cannot be expected to furnish the same variety of incidents as that of a warrior or a statesman, though the civil virtues and splendid talents of Leonardo da Vinci were probably more useful to his country than the warlike qualifications of his more ambitious contemporaries, which were usually accompanied by violence and followed by remorse.

Leonardo da Vinci had now reached his thirty-first year, and was most indefatigable in the study of whatever might tend to his improvement or increase his knowledge in the art of painting, to which he almost

exclusively devoted himself.   One of his first undertakings was the celebrated " Cartone," pasteboard or
rather thick paper, which he designed, by the orders
of the King of Portugal, for a piece of tapestry that
was to be worked in Flanders for that monarch.   This
drawing represented the story of Adam and Eve when
first tempted to sin, and surpassed every thing which
had been seen of the kind.

One of his first pictures was a painting of the Madonna, in which he introduced, among other acces-
sories, a vase of flowers, so inimitably executed that
the dew seemed glittering on the leaves.   This production became afterwards the property of Pope Clement the Seventh, who purchased it at an immense
price.   For his friend Antonio Segni he formed a
design of Neptune drawn in his car by sea-horses
through the ocean, surrounded by Tritons, Mermaids,
and all the other attributes of that deity which his
fertile imagination could invent.   It was some time
after presented by Segni's son, Fabio, to Messer Giovanni Gaddi, with this epigram :—

" Pinxit Virgilius Neptunum : pinxit Homerus
    Dum maris undisoni per vada flectit equos :
    Mente quidem vates illum conspexit uterque ;
    Vincius est oculis, jureque vincit eos."

Da Vinci always took great pleasure in delineating
the most grotesque figures and extraordinary faces, so
that, if he met a man in the street with any peculiarity
of ugliness or deformity of countenance, he would
follow him until he had a correct idea of his face, and
would then draw the person, on his return home, from
memory, as well as if he had been present.   He not

only studied to perfect himself in giving the mere
beauty or deformity of the likenesses he painted, but
he sought to give the very air, manner, and expression
of the persons represented.   He at all times preferred
studying from nature to following rules that were then
but imperfectly understood ; and he was in the habit
of inviting the contadini, and people of the lower
orders, to sup with him, telling them the most ridiculous stories, that he might delineate the natural expressions of rude delight undisguised by the refinements of good breeding.   He would then show them
their own likenesses, which no one could possibly
behold without laughter at the ridiculous faces which
he had caricatured, but with so much truth that the
originals could not be mistaken.*   He was so indefatigable in pursuing the object of his ambition, that
he neglected no means of procuring fresh studies
for his pencil.   He would sometimes put himself to
the pain of accompanying criminals to the place of
execution, and would remain with them in their last
moments, that he might catch the expression of their
countenances, and delineate the agony of their sufferings.   In short, there was no branch of his art which
he considered unworthy of his attention, aware that
perfection in any thing is only to be attained by un-
wearied industry and application.   We find from
Vasari, that it was about this time that he painted a
picture for the Grand Duke Cosimo the First, representing an angel in strong light and shade, which was

* The best of these caricatures were published by Clarke, in
1786, from drawings by Wenceslaus Hollar, taken from the
Portland Museum.

placed by that prince in the collection of the "Palazzo Vecchio," from whence it had been missing for upwards of a century. Most probably it was turned out of its place from the oversight or carelessness of the directors, who had condemned it to be put aside with a quantity of rubbish, old furniture and frames, which are occasionally sold by order of the Duke's guardaroba. It was not long since bought by a "rivenditore" for twenty-one quatrini, about three pence, and resold to its present possessor, the Signore Fineschi, a drawing-master of Florence, for five pauls, two shillings and sixpence. There is no doubt of the originality of this painting, both from the particular style of colouring Leonardo made use of, and the sort of stucco with which it is covered behind, a chemical composition which he is well known to have used to preserve his pictures from the worms when they were painted on wood. It is also most accurately described in Vasari's Life of Leonardo, in these words:—" Among the best things in the Duke Cosimo's palace is the head of an angel with one arm lifted up in the air, shortened off about the elbow, and the other with the hand on the bosom. It is a very extraordinary thing that this great genius was in the habit of seeking for the very darkest blacks, in order to effect a sort of chiaro scuro, which added more brilliancy to his pictures, and gave them more the appearance of night than the clearness of day; but this was in order to increase the relief, and so improve the art of painting."

The celebrated picture of the Medusa's head, which is now in the Public Gallery at Florence, was executed about this time, but, as it was a work that required great labour, it, like too many of his undertakings, is in an unfinished state. It is a most extraordinary subject, and the snakes are interwoven and grouped together instead of hair with such wonderful skill, that it excites almost as much disgust as admiration.

The fame of Leonardo's extraordinary abilities spread through Italy, and he was invited by several princes to reside at their courts, and enrich their palaces with his works. The example of the great Lorenzo had raised an emulation among the princes of Italy for the encouragement of literary men ; and whoever was distinguished by talent was sure not only of wealth and preferment, but was flattered and caressed by all his superiors. The unusual tranquillity Italy enjoyed from the wise precautions and conciliatory policy of Lorenzo de' Medici, left her turbulent rulers at leisure to cultivate the arts of peace. Their habitual restlessness required employment; and reduced to inaction by the temporary cessation of their petty wars and intrigues, their ambition consisted in drawing to their respective courts the greatest men of that luminous period. Lorenzo may therefore be justly styled not only the Mæcenas of Florence, which he governed, but of the age in which he lived, as his politics so materially influenced the revival of literature and the progress of general civilization.

Anxious to secure to himself a certain provision for his expensive style of living, Leonardo addressed a letter to Ludovico Sforza, surnamed *Il Moro*, offering his services to that prince, who governed Milan during his nephew's minority, and whom he knew to be most desirous of attracting to his court all the *literati* of the age, under the pretence of assisting him in the young

Duke's education.* None of the writers of that period have given any reason why Leonardo preferred the patronage of Ludovico to that of the house of Medici, particularly as the latter were distinguished by their liberal encouragement of the arts. Perhaps Lorenzo might have sent him to *Il Moro*, with whom he was in strict alliance, or Leonardo might have preferred Milan himself, where he would have hoped to have found a more extensive field for the exercise of his talents, and less competition than he must have had to contend with at Florence. The uncertainty of his birth perhaps influenced so high minded a man; and he probably wished to establish his own fortunes at a strange court, where he was only known as an illustrious Florentine distinguished by his sovereign for the superiority of his talents and acquirements. Whatever might have been Da Vinci's motive, it is certain that he entered the service of the Duke of Milan, and consented to receive an annual salary of five hundred scudi, which was then by no means a contemptible sum. He was, moreover, entitled to various privileges and immunities, and permitted to appropriate to his own use the produce of such of his paintings as were not executed by the Duke's order.

It is important to the history of Leonardo da Vinci to fix, as nearly as possible, the period of his arrival at Milan. From the most authentic sources it appears that he must have taken up his residence there pre-

---

* It is a curious fact, that Leonardo da Vinci always wrote from right to left, like the Persians, for which no one has been able to account. It was most probably a love of singularity; and, although it increases the difficulty of deciphering his manuscripts, it also serves to place their identity beyond dispute.

vious to the year 1487; for we find in an old treatise
entitled "Della Luce e dell' Ombra," in his own
hand-writing, the following observation: "A dì 23
d' Aprile 1490, chominciai questo libro, e richominciai
il Cavallo." * In this memorandum he no doubt
alludes to the equestrian statue of Francesco Sforza
the First, which, if he recommenced in 1490, he must
have begun long before, as it must have consumed
much time to form the necessary moulds and designs.
Moreover, he is alluded to by Belincionni, a Florentine
poet, who resided at the court of Ludovico il Moro,
and celebrated most of the principal events of that
period, under the name of the " Apelle Fiorentino : "

> " Quì come l' ape al miel viene ogni dotto,
>   Di virtuosi ha la sua corte piena :
>   Da Fiorenza un Apelle ha quì condotto ;" &c. †

and the editor Tantio, or Tanzi, has added in the
margin, fearing it might not be understood, " Magistro
Leonardo da Vinci."

There is also another authority not less respectable
than the former, in the Ricordi of Monsignore Sabba
da Castiglione, which dates his coming to Milan as far
back as 1483, from the circumstance of his having
been an eye-witness to the destruction of this unfinished equestrian statue, when the French under
Charles the Eighth took possession of Milan, in 1499.
There is no evidence to confirm the assertion of this

---

* " On the 23rd of April, 1490, I began this book, and recommenced the horse."

† " Like bees to hive, here flocks each learned sage,
    With all that 's great and good his court is throng'd :
    From Florence fair hath an Apelles come," &c.

noble Milanese writer that his contemporary Leonardo
had worked at this model for sixteen years ; but there
is no reason to disbelieve him when he declares he saw
the bowmen of Gascony make use of this magnificent
production as a target.

Ludovico il Moro, at whose request Leonardo went
to the court of Milan, although only nominally Regent,
governed that state with absolute authority ; for his
nephew, Giovan Galeazzo, possessed merely the title,
and enjoyed the pageantry of sovereignty, without the
slightest power.

Ludovico Sforza, surnamed " Il Moro," not from
his darkness of complexion, as is erroneously stated
by Gibbon, but from his having taken a mulberry-tree,
in Italian " Moro," for his device,* was a prince of
great talents, and one of the first politicians of the
age.   Although the more noble qualities of his mind
were obscured by ambition, he was greatly beloved
by all who were about his person, and admitted to his
intimate society.   He was frank and pleasing in his
manners, easy of access, and liberal even to profusion
to those who possessed his confidence.   To a very
handsome and prepossessing exterior he united the
most powerful eloquence.   He successfully cultivated

---

* " The Signore Ludovico Sforza, Duke of Milan, adopted
a mulberry-tree, Moro, as his device, from its being considered
wiser than all other trees, as it buds later, and does not flower
until it has escaped the injuries of winter, when it immediately
bears fruit: thereby demonstrating itself of a nature to do nothing hastily, but rather maturely to reflect, and then promptly
execute.   This wise prince made use of this device as emblematic
of a similarity of disposition."—See Giovio, *Vite d'Uomini
Illustri.*

the arts of peace, and lost no opportunity of drawing to his court those who had most distinguished themselves in the arts and sciences. It was his opinion that much more might be done by council than by arms; and that the pen was frequently of more weight than the sword; he was therefore averse to warlike enterprises, and always preferred obtaining his object by overreaching his adversaries in politics and intrigue. To such a man Leonardo da Vinci must have been invaluable. His various talents, to a prince who so well knew how to appreciate them, were of the greatest importance, and he was received at his court with every possible demonstration of favour and affection. It would far exceed the limits of this work to enumerate all the celebrated men whom Ludovico had drawn around him under the laudable pretence of his nephew's instruction and amusement. The poet Belincionni has enumerated them in his various compositions; and Leonardo is also mentioned in most honourable terms.

" Del Vinci e suoi pennelli e suoi colori,
I moderni e gli antichi hanno paura."*

The Padre Luca Paciolo, who was the friend and companion of Leonardo and the great restorer of mathematics in Italy, places our hero before all his contemporaries, and makes the following playful allusion to his name : " Il Vince in scoltura, getto, e pittura, con ciascuna il nome verifica." †

Vasari is greatly mistaken in supposing that Ludo-

* Vinci and his pencils and his colours, both moderns and ancients have in dread.

† " Vinci in sculpture, casts, and painting, verifies his name with all."

vico sent for Da Vinci merely to amuse him with his
musical talents ; * for it appears very improbable that
this prince, who was so well aware of Leonardo's
knowledge and taste for the fine arts, from having the
famous " Rotella del Fico" in his possession, which
was painted by him when a young man, should have
considered him in the light of a musician. Whatever
reputation he might have gained for playing on the
lyre, it is evident that he himself considered that
accomplishment a mere pastime, as he never makes
the slightest mention of his musical abilities in the
celebrated letter addressed by him to the Duke of
Milan : and if the enlightened politics and vast ideas
of Ludovico il Moro are considered, it will be readily
conceived that Leonardo was sent for with the view of
giving instruction to others as well as of working himself, by instituting an academy of arts and sciences,
of which he was to have the chief direction. We
know also from the best historians of the period, that
this wary prince, from the moment of his brother
Galeazzo Maria's assassination, had formed the plan
of usurping his throne, and therefore was particularly
anxious to draw over to his party the most celebrated
men in Italy ; as the protection and patronage of such

* "It is true that he was an excellent musician and a particularly
good performer on the lyre; so much so, that Lommazo reputes
him superior to every one in that art. A note is to be seen in
his Codex, marked Q. R. p. 28, where a new viola is mentioned
of his construction ; and in another place there is a drawing by
him for a lyre. Vasari speaks of a lyre which belonged to him
in the form of a horse's head, the greatest part of which was
silver; and I saw his portrait done with a guitar in his hand for
the frontispiece of an old parchment manuscript dedicated to
Cardinal Ascanio Sforza." See Ammoretti.

eminent persons could not fail to increase his reputation and strengthen his power. The advantage of
such a mode of proceeding had been already seen in
the popularity of the Medici at Florence, and of his
own ancestors the Visconti at Milan. That painting
was never neglected in Lombardy, is shown by the
Abbate Lanzi, in his "Storia Pittorica," in which he
observes, that "while the whole of Europe was obscured by the grossest ignorance, Lombardy still preserved the use, and cultivated a general taste for
the art of painting, of which there are several monuments still existing; amongst others the church of
Galiano, about six miles to the south of Como, painted
in the year 1007."

When Giotto came to Milan, which undoubtedly
was previous to 1334, to paint the Visconti palace,
that art assumed a superior character, and created a
school which has produced many great men, whose
works are still preserved in some of the ancient
churches and in the private collections of several individuals. There is a lasting monument of the revival
of sculpture in the church of San Francesco, done in
the year 1316, representing the transit of the Blessed
Virgin, in marble, and two other monuments, the work
of Giovanni da Pisa, finished in 1339. The improvement of architecture may be dated from the time
when Gian Galeazzo Visconti invited the first masters
to Milan in order to construct the cathedral; but they
had not then abandoned the Gothic style. The Abbate
Lanzi's work just cited, will show the progress made
in the arts and sciences until the arrival of Leonardo;
but a great deal is to be gathered from the inedited

Memoirs of the Painters, Sculptors, and Architects of Milan, by the late Antonio Albuzzi.

Leonardo now found himself in possession of what was then considered an affluent fortune, which relieved his mind from the consideration of being obliged to provide for his own support. He found Ludovico an easy patron, and was much delighted with his situation. Caressed and flattered by the whole court, he entered with all the energy of his character into the pleasures and amusements of the gay world, and made almost daily progress in the confidence and good opinion of Ludovico, by flattering his wishes and sharing his amusements. By turns a poet, a painter, a musician, and always a most accomplished courtier, he completely gained Il Moro's favour, who, although a crafty politician and a man of sense, was, nevertheless, open to flattery, and unable to resist the fascinations of such versatile talents. Ludovico was a great lover of pleasure, and was almost as much distinguished by the dissolute intrigues and lascivious amours of his private life, as by the sagacity and steadiness of his public conduct; and whilst Da Vinci assisted at his councils, and adorned the city with public buildings, he likewise painted his mistresses, and diverted his leisure hours with music and poetry; in short, he was always ready either for his patron's service or pleasure.

The first public work in which Leonardo was employed after his arrival at Milan, was the celebrated equestrian statue of Francesco Sforza the First, which, if we may believe the authority before cited of Monsignore Sabba da Castiglione, he began in 1483. According to the poet Taccone, it would have been

sooner commenced had any one been found capable of
undertaking it :—

> " E se più presto non s' è principiato,
>   La voglia del Signore fu sempre pronta :
>   Non s'era un Leonardo ancor trovato,
>   Che di presente tanto ben l'impronta," &c.*

From the high opinion entertained of his taste, Leonardo was made director of all the public fêtes and
entertainments either given by the sovereign, or to
him by the lords of his court; of which Belincionni
has preserved the recollection in the poems written by
him on these occasions; and if Tantio, who collected
and published them, has observed a proper chronolo-
gical order, we may date the two representations in
praise of Patience and Labour, given by the Sanse-
verini family in honour of the nuptials of Isabella and
Beatrice, to the first year of his residence at Milan.
To this period we may also refer Leonardo's celebrated
portraits of Ludovico's two favourites, Cecilia Gallerani and Lucrezia Crevelli, so frequently celebrated
by the poets of that age.

Belincionni's sonnet on the picture of the former
does more honour to the painter than the poet :

> " Di che t' adiri, a chi invidia hai Natura!
>   Al Vinci che ha ritratto una tua stella.
>   Cecilia sì, bellissima, oggi è quella
>   Che a' suoi begli occhi, il sol par ombra oscura.
> L' onor é tuo, sebben con sua pittura
>   La fa che par che ascolti, e non favella.

---

* " And if this work was not sooner begun,
  The sovereign's will was always ready,
  But a Leonardo had not then been found,
  Who at this time so well undertakes it."

Pensa quanto sarà più viva e bella,
Più a te fia gloria nell' età futura.
Ringraziar dunque Lodovico, or puoi,
E l' ingegno e la man di Leonardo
Che a' posteri di lei voglion far parte.
Che lei vedra così, benchè sia tardo,
Vederla viva dirà : basti à noi
Comprender or quella, ch' è natura ed arte."

This portrait was at Milan at the end of the last century, in the Marchese Bonesana's collection, and
there is a fine old copy in the Public Gallery. The
Gallerani married Count Ludovico Pergamino; she
was a lady of very great talents, and a poetess. Da
Vinci painted one of his best pictures for her, representing the Virgin and Child in the act of blessing one
of those roses, vulgarly called " Rose della Madonna;"
and this picture was in the possession of a wine-mer-
chant at Milan when the French occupied that city
during the late war. It is framed in the fashion of
those times, with a scroll bearing this inscription :

" Per Cecilia qual te orna, lauda, e adora
E'l tuo unico figlio, o beata Vergine exora! "

The portrait of Lucrezia Crevelli, which was not less
celebrated and admired than that of her fair contemporary, is now in the Louvre at Paris.

The greatest proof of the esteem and consideration
in which Il Moro must have held Leonardo, not only
as a painter, sculptor, and mechanic, but also as a
man well versed in all the arts and sciences, is his
having chosen him to be the founder and director of
the academy he caused to be established. The Padre
Luca Paciolo informs us, that that prince had long
been desirous of forming a union of learned men and

skilful artists, who might reciprocally communicate their knowledge, and forward the progress of literature and the arts. That such an academy existed at Milan, the first that was ever known in that city, and to which Leonardo gave his name, is proved by the testimony of Vasari, and by several manuscripts still existing in the Ambrosian Library, and also by six engravings representing several ingenious devices, in the centre of which is inscribed " Academia Leonardi Vinci."

It is most probable, that for the use of this academy, and for the purpose of argument with his colleagues and instruction to his pupils, Leonardo wrote all those tracts which are to be found, not only in his " Trattato della Pittura," but in several manuscript volumes which are now preserved in the Public Gallery at Milan. This would easily explain his reasons for undertaking so many and such various arguments ; and would also account for the number of unconnected ideas, unfinished sketches, memoranda, and materials for the composition of future works, as well as several complete and highly finished discourses. Among the latter, his " Trattato della Pittura," is generally considered as one of his best and most useful compositions ; so much so that the Count Algarotti has not hesitated to declare, that even in the present day he should not desire any better elementary work on the art of painting ; an opinion entertained by many other distinguished writers.

Although it is now almost impossible to fix the exact epoch of the foundation of the Vincean academy, it must have been about the year 1485 or 1486, as, previous to that time, we know that Leonardo was engaged in forming the model of the equestrian statue of Francesco Sforza, and afterwards in painting the two portraits of Ludovico's mistresses which have been mentioned.

In 1489 we find Da Vinci occupied by his patron's orders in preparing a grand fête which was to be given in celebration of the young Duke Giovan Galeazzo's marriage with Isabella of Arragon. For this entertainment he invented a moving representation of the planets, which, as they approached the royal party in their evolutions, opened of themselves, and discovered a person dressed to represent the deity attributed to each planet, who recited verses composed by Belincionni in honour of the occasion.* We also learn from an old manuscript, in which there is a memorandum in his hand-writing, that he invented and directed a sort of joust, or tournament, given by Messer Galeazzo da Sanseverino to the Duke and his court; which he incidentally mentions from the circumstance of his servant Jachomo having committed a theft on the occasion.

In 1492, Il Moro having formed a plan to turn the waters of the Ticino, in order to fertilize the country to the right of that river, had recourse to Leonardo's knowledge of hydraulics to carry his intentions into execution. We know from his notes, that about that time he visited Sesto Calende, Varal pombio, and

---

* The reader will find an account of these fêtes in the Ricordi of Monsignore da Castiglione ; and Belincionni's verses are included in his works, collected and published by Tantio, at Milan, in 1495, which are now extremely scarce.

Vegevano, where " ai 20 di Marzo del 1492," he observes that " nella vernata le vigne si sotterano."

In this manner Ludovico continued to avail himself of Da Vinci's various talents, and kept him constantly employed, not only as a painter, but also in superintending the magnificent entertainments given either by himself or his nobles, in directing the public works, and in ornamenting his palaces.*

It is generally supposed that Leonardo first introduced the art of engraving on wood and copper, and that the designs of several old plates, representing the most celebrated literary men at Ludovico's court, were of his composition. It is also said that these were the first examples of an author's portrait being prefixed to his works, unless we credit Pliny's account that the Romans were accustomed to make use of engravings on wood. His beautiful picture of the Virgin and Child with St John and St. Michael, now in possession of Count San Vitale, of Parma, is dated in that year; and, what is almost without example

---

* To give some idea of the manner in which the Hall of the Castle of Milan was painted, and of the prices in those days, the following note is transcribed, viz.

" The narrow border round the top of the room, 30 lire. The moulding underneath, each square separately, 7 do.; and the expense of blue, gold, bistre, indigo, and gum, 3 do. Three days' labour.—Pictures under the pannels, 12 lire each. Each of the arches, 7 lire. The cornice under the windows, 6 soldi the brace. For 24 stories from the Roman History, 10 lire. An ounce of blue, 10 soldi. Gold, 15 soldi. Black, 2½ do. Five days' labour in the composition," &c. &c.

N. B. The Italian lira is about 8½d. English, and the soldo is as nearly as possible a French sous.

in his works, is inscribed, "Leonardo Vinci fece, 1492."

About the end of the autumn in 1494, Charles the Eighth invaded Italy, and repaired to Pavia, where Il Moro had prepared the most magnificent fêtes and entertainments for his reception, and the arrangement of the whole was entrusted to the elegant taste of Leonardo da Vinci.

During his residence at Pavia, Leonardo, who never permitted any opportunity to escape him by which he could acquire information, determined to employ his time in studying the anatomy of the human frame under the instructions of Marc' Antonio della Torre, a learned Genoese, and one of the most celebrated professors of that university. These two great men were equally pleased with each other ; the professor deriving much benefit from the correct drawings Leonardo executed to illustrate their studies, and the latter being greatly improved by the thorough knowledge of the human frame which he thus acquired.

It was always Da Vinci's opinion that a perfect acquaintance with anatomy was essentially necessary to a painter, and that without it he could not hope to attain any excellence in his art,—a doctrine which he has enforced in a manuscript now existing in the Ambrosian Library at Milan. " It is necessary that a painter should be a good anatomist, that in his attitudes and gestures he may be able to design the naked parts of the human frame, according to the just rules of the anatomy of the nerves, bones, and muscles ; and that in his different positions he may know what particular nerve or muscle is the cause of such a particular movement, in order that he may make that

only marked and apparent, and not all the rest, as
many artists are in the habit of doing ; who, that they
may appear great designers, make the naked limbs
stiff and without grace, so that they have more the
appearance of a bag of nuts than the human superficies,
or rather more like a bundle of radishes than naked
muscles."

In this manner Leonardo and his learned instructor
pursued their studies together, deriving equal advantage from the exertion of their respective talents. Da
Vinci used to draw the naked parts of the human frame
in red chalk; while his friend described them with
such admirable skill,. that Vasari declares he was the
first who brought the science of anatomy into general
repute, by rendering it plain to all. Some of these
drawings are preserved in the Royal Library in London, as the celebrated Dr. Hunter, in his course of
Anatomical Lectures published in 1784, mentions
having seen them, and greatly admires the precision
with which they are executed, particularly in the most
minute parts of the muscles.

From Pavia Charles, still accompanied by Ludovico
and his court, repaired to Piacenza, and there soon
after received intelligence of Giovan-Galeazzo's death.
This occasioned Il Moro's immediate return to Milan ;
when the Ducal Council, privately suborned, decreed
that the crown should be confirmed to him in preference to Giovan-Galeazzo's infant children, as they
considered it necessary to the general good to place
the government in the hands of a powerful prince,
who could defend the state and provide for its security
amidst the broils and misfortunes which threatened the
tranquillity of Italy.

In the mean time Leonardo had returned to Milan from Pavia, where he left his friend Marc' Antonio della Torre, and recommenced his exertions for his patron Ludovico, who, now firmly established as Duke of Milan by the voice of the people, the connivance of the French King, and the Emperor's grant, had greater leisure for the cultivation of the fine arts. He was a prince of quiet habits, mild in his manners, and particularly averse to bloodshed—so much so, that we may doubt his having been at all concerned in his nephew's death. In order to gain the favour of the people, he amused them with continual entertainments, and collected around him the greatest men from all parts of Italy, who by their talents and accomplishments might contribute to the embellishment of his city, or the refinements of his court. The poet, the historian, and the painter, equally shared his patronage, and were equally zealous in their demonstrations of gratitude. The court of Milan became what that of Florence had ceased to be; the latter being desolated by internal broils, the arts of peace fled to a more congenial soil, and Ludovico was now the great patron of the fine arts, and the restorer of literature in Italy.

Shortly after his return to Milan, Leonardo was called upon to celebrate the Duke's virtues, and designed a picture of which we find a description in his own writing: " Il Moro representing Fortune, with flowing hair and his hands extended, and Messer Gualtiere in the act of doing homage to him in the foreground; Poverty in frightful guise is pursuing a youth whom Il Moro is sheltering under his robe, while with his golden rod he menaces the monster, and warns him not to approach."

c 2

From several memoranda and remarks which are to
be found among his manuscripts, such as, "A dì 24
Marzo 1494, venne Galeazzo a stare meco, con il
patto di dare 5 lire il mese, pagando ogni 14 dì del
mese. Datemi da suo padre fiorini due di Reno;"
and a little lower down, " A dì 14 di Luglio ebbe da
Galeazzo fiorini 2 di Reno,"—it is evident he was in
the habit of receiving scholars who paid him for the
benefit they derived from his instructions, and the
information they gained by frequenting his studio.

In the year 1495 there is no mention of any particular work having been undertaken by Leonardo. It
is most probable that he was occupied in perfecting
the Vincian Academy ; as it is supposed he wrote his
famous Treatise addressed to the Duke about this
time, in which he examines the respective merits of
the two arts, painting and sculpture. It is much to
be lamented that this book is no longer extant, as it
would have been highly interesting to know the opinion of one so capable of forming a proper judgment
from his extensive knowledge of the fine arts. Leonardo's treatise was composed for the use of the Academy, and is even now held in general estimation. In
the collection of his works lately published at Paris,
there are several tracts comparing the different merits
of the sister arts, both considered relatively and individually, which prove that this treatise really existed;
and it is moreover frequently alluded to in the " Trattato della Pittura," written by Lomazzo, who was his
friend and scholar.

Leonardo's pencil was not, however, unemployed
during this year, as the Duke ordered him to paint
his own and the Duchess's portraits on each side of a

large picture representing Mount Calvary, which Montorfani had painted on the wall of the refectory in the Convento delle Grazie. This task he very unwillingly undertook, if we may believe Padre Gattico, a Dominican friar, who has left an account of this convent in manuscript, in which he says : " Quelle pitture si sono infradiciate per essere dipinte all' olio, perchè l' olio non si conserva in pitture fatte sopra mure e pietra." * About the end of this year, a curious work was printed at Milan on music, by Franchino Gaforio, which was preceded by an engraving, supposed to have been done by Leonardo, or by one of his scholars under his direction and with his assistance.

In the year 1496, Da Vinci derived much pleasure from the arrival of his friend and countryman the Padre Luca Paciolo, who has been before mentioned in these pages. As they had studied together, and were equally well versed in mechanics, mathematics, and architecture, they were mutually delighted with each other's society, and Leonardo had sufficient influence with the Duke to persuade him to receive his friend into his service. Engaged in the same pursuits, they lived in the same house, shared the same studies and amusements, and assisted each other in their separate undertakings. Paciolo prevailed on his friend to draw all the geometrical figures for his Treatise on Architecture, as he well knew there was no one capable of executing them with the same precision ; and he acknowledges this assistance in the following well-merited eulogium : " As in the disposition of the

* " These pictures have mouldered away in consequence of their being painted in oil, because oil does not keep in paintings made upon walls and stone."

regular bodies, you will observe those which are done
by that most worthy painter, architect, musician, and
universally endowed Leonardo da Vinci, a Florentine,
at the city of Milan, when we were both in the pay of
the most excellent Duke Ludovico Maria Sforza, in
the year of our salvation 1496."

A little further on he mentions the drawings which
Leonardo made for his work on the "Divina propor-
tione," which he dedicated in manuscript to the Duke
Ludovico. They were sixty in number, and were
published in 1509, with a new dedication to Pietro
Soderini, Gonfaloniere of Florence, to whom he writes :
" Libellum .... Ludovico Sportiæ nuncupavi tanto
ardore, quoque sua Vincii nostri Lionardi manibus
scalpta," &c.

To this period also belongs the drawings, or rather
illustrations, of the celebrated " Codice Triulziano,"
which was written by the Duke's eldest son, Maximilian, when a child studying the Latin language. This
manuscript forms a small quarto volume written on
parchment, which, besides being ornamented with
numerous highly finished devices and heraldic embla-
zonments, is enriched with several pictures relating to
the youth and occupations of the young prince, who
then possessed the title of Count of Pavia. Among
these there are two which are generally considered
the production of Leonardo's pencil : one representing
the Count in the act of doing homage to his cousin
the Emperor Maximilian; and the other, of the same
prince amusing himself catching birds, while his tutor,
Count Secco di Borella, is advising him to leave off
his diversions and attend to his studies. This manuscript is held in the greatest estimation, and is still
preserved at Milan.

About the end of this year Ludovico il Moro went to Pavia, attended by all his court, to meet the Emperor Maximilian, whom he had invited into Italy. Triumphal arches were prepared everywhere on his road, and most magnificent fêtes awaited his arrival wherever he stopped; as Ludovico disguised his true reason for this conference under the pretence of merely doing homage to his feudal lord. Leonardo, who accompanied his patron on this occasion, had no doubt a principal share in arranging these festivities. That he was not forgotten by the Duke is proved by his having ordered him to paint a picture of the Nativity, which he presented to the Emperor in honour of the occasion, and which is now in the Imperial cabinet at Vienna.

Leonardo's residence at the court of Milan, although extremely agreeable to himself, was highly detrimental to his fame as a painter; as he was so constantly occupied in different works for the good of the state and the amusement of the court, that he could not devote so much of his time to painting as his admirers wish. A number of those pictures which are really his own, are left in an unfinished state, from the extreme nicety of his taste. His imagination went so far beyond what it is in the power of man to execute, that he was seldom or ever contented with his own works, and he would frequently lay aside a picture altogether, if it did not equal his ideas of the subject. At other times he would hastily abandon an undertaking, if his design did not embrace all that his imagination had preconceived. Hence there remain so few pictures by this inimitable artist; but these few are so very highly finished, that no one since has been

supposed to have surpassed him.   Many of the pictures
which are shown in Italy as Leonardo's paintings, are
falsely considered so, ~~particularly in Milan~~, where they
are generally the work of some of his scholars, with
the advantage of receiving the last touches from
himself.

There could have been no part of Da Vinci's life
more pleasant to himself than the time he spent at
Milan previous to the misfortunes of the house of
Sforza.   In the full enjoyment of his princely patron's
confidence and favour, he lived in the most splendid
manner, beloved and respected by every body.   Free
from all care for present wants, and too little accustomed to consider the future, he passed his time in
the gratification of his favourite pursuits, and devoted
his leisure to the entertainment of his friends.   Expensive in his habits, he kept a most liberal table; his
house was always open to whoever was distinguished
for talents or accomplishments; and he drew around
him the best society in Milan during that brilliant
period.   He sought for merit wherever it was to be
found, for the rust of envy never corroded his noble
heart, and the poorest artist was always welcome to a
seat at his board and a share of his purse.

His principal object in life was the encouragement
of literature and the arts, in all their various branches;
and, enthusiastically desirous of promoting what he
most loved, he assisted the poor, encouraged the weak,
and brought forward the unknown.   It is only to be
regretted that his means did not equal his inclinations;
for his profuse liberality rendered him but ill qualified
to give assistance to others; and unfortunately his
friend and patron Ludovico il Moro had exactly the

same propensities. He also undertook more than
he was capable of finishing ; his ideas were too much
enlarged for his situation, which impoverished his
treasury, diminished his revenues, and became the
principal cause of his ultimate ruin. A proper attention to his expenditure is as necessary to a prince as
to an individual, without which, even with the very
best intentions, neither can be certain of remaining
honest. The one must oppress his subjects, the other
must defraud his equals; and both must risk the loss
of that claim to assistance in the hour of need which
both may occasionally require. Upon no one was this
truth more severely impressed than on Ludovico il
Moro, who, although he had exhausted his finances in
beautifying his city and encouraging the arts, was
neglected by his subjects when they found he had exhausted his resources; and they left him to pay the
forfeit of his imprudence and ambition with the loss of
his dominions and his life.

On his return to Milan from Pavia, the Duke was
desirous of enriching his capital with some great work
that should be considered worthy of Da Vinci's talents,
and serve to perpetuate the fame of the artist and the
liberality of the prince. With this idea Ludovico desired Leonardo to paint his celebrated picture of " The
Last Supper," on the walls of the refectory in the
Dominican Convent of the " Madonna delle Grazie."

It was almost impossible to have selected a subjec
more adapted to Leonardo's taste and genius, and he
had certainly never before undertaken so interesting a
work. He proposed to represent the moment when
our Saviour exclaims " Amen dico vobis quia unus
vestrûm me traditurus est." This gave him an oppor-

tunity of exercising his peculiar talent, of representing the different passions that agitate the human frame, and of giving to each individual of his picture the merit and interest of a separate composition, without disturbing the harmony of the whole.

It is not exactly known when he commenced this picture, but from various circumstances it appears that it must have been about the year 1497, as Bottari tells us there is a rude engraving bearing that date, and supposed to be Leonardo's own work. The Padre Luca Paciolo mentions, in one of his manuscripts, that in 1498 Leonardo had already considerably advanced in drawing the outlines of this composition; and who- ever observes it now, at least as much as is spared to us from the ravages of time and the attacks of ignor- ance, will easily perceive that three or even four years are very little to have employed on such an under- taking; the more so when we consider Leonardo's extreme difficulty in being satisfied with his own pro- ductions. It is also to be remembered, that he was obliged to form a cartoon of the same size as his picture.

The general disposition of this admirable work is considered extremely simple, and therefore the more appropriate to the subject. Our Saviour is repre- sented seated in the middle, which is the place of honour: his attitude is tranquil and majestic, a kind of noble serenity appears to pervade his countenance and action, which impresses respect. The Apostles, on the contrary, are in extreme agitation, and their attitudes and countenances are expressive of various emotions. Fear, love, anxiety, and a desire to pene- trate the full extent of our Saviour's meaning, are easily distinguishable in their looks and gestures. But when Leonardo wished to pourtray the character of the divinity on the figure and countenance of our Lord, his hand was too weak to represent the conceptions of his mind, and whatever he executed was still very far from satisfying the sublimity and delicacy of his ideas. At length, despairing of success, he unburthened his mind to his friend Bernardo Zenale,* who, not believing that he could surpass what he had already done, advised him to leave the head of Christ unfinished. Leonardo, after much consideration, resolved to follow his friend's counsel: in imitation of Timanthes, of whom it is related, that in his picture of the Sacrifice of Iphigenia, having employed every possible expression of grief in the attendants, he conceived he could not do more justice to the father's feelings, who was to behold the sacrifice of his own child, than by covering his face with his mantle, and leaving the effect to the beholder's imagination.†

Nothing can be more impressive than the idea of the impossibility of representing our Saviour's countenance by human means; and this very imperfection becomes a greater beauty in a country where one is too much accustomed to see the Deity represented, or rather misrepresented, in all sorts of extraordinary and fantastic forms, in the old frescoes and mosaics.‡

* This painter and architect was a native of Treviso, and was working at the same time as Leonardo in the Convent of the " Madonna delle Grazie." Lomazzo mentions him as the author of a treatise on Perspective, of which he had a thorough knowledge. See Lomazzo *Idea del Tempio della Pittura*, book 5, chap. 21.

† Plin. lib. 35, cap. 10.

‡ As an example of the paintings alluded to, it is sufficient to

Having settled this difficulty, he found himself speedily embarrassed by another, which was to find a countenance sufficiently wicked to convey an idea of the man who was about to betray his divine master. This feeling, to one who was always in the habit of long reflection before he attempted any thing of consequence, greatly delayed his work, and gave rise to the story Vasari tells of the Prior of the Dominicans, who became impatient whenever he saw Leonardo in contemplation instead of continuing his picture; he being one of those who imagine that a painter must be neglecting his work whenever his hands are not actually employed on it. He therefore complained of Leonardo's indolence to the Duke, who, in order to satisfy him, inquired about the picture, and found that the artist never passed a day without working at it at least for two hours. Still, however, its progress did not keep pace with the Prior's impatience, who continued to persecute the Duke with his complaints until he prevailed on him to send for Da Vinci, and remonstrate with him on his delay. But Ludovico did this with so much kindness and affability that Leonardo was quite charmed with the prince's condescension, and willingly explained to him, that a man of genius is, in fact, never less occupied than when he appears to be entirely so, particularly in painting, where so much depends on a just and proper conception of the subject. He concluded by telling the Duke, " There remain, Sir, only two heads unfinished in the whole

mention an old picture on wood of the Annunciation, in which the Almighty is represented as an old man looking in at the window, while the angel is delivering the divine message to the Virgin,

picture. That of Christ I have long despaired of ever being able to complete, as I am quite convinced of the utter impossibility of finding a model on earth capable of representing the union of divinity with humanity, and much less can I hope to supply the deficiency from my own imagination. Nothing therefore is wanting but to express the character of Judas, and I have for some time sought without success, among your prisons and the very refuse of the people, for a countenance such as I require ; but if your Excellency is so impatient that the picture should be finished, I can take the likeness of the Dominican Prior, who richly deserves it for the impertinence of his interference." The Duke could not avoid laughing heartily at this sally, and being fully convinced how much labour and judgment Leonardo bestowed on each individual, was only impressed with a still greater respect for his talents. It may also be easily supposed that the fear of being handed down to posterity as Judas, effectually silenced the Prior's importunities.* Da Vinci, however, was a man of too much honour to have had any idea of putting his threat in execution, as has been erroneously asserted ; besides which, the Prior of the Dominicans is described by the writers of that period as having too noble an appearance for such a purpose. Some little time after, Leonardo found a face such as he required, so that by adding something from his imagination, he finished the head of Judas, completed his picture, and excelled all his former productions.

In this wonderful composition, which was then con-

* This story is to be found in Bottari's " Lettere Pittoriche," and its truth is confirmed by Vasari and several of Leonardo da Vinci's contemporaries.

sidered almost a miracle of human perfection, Leonardo derived the greatest assistance from his previous
studies. These he found a perfect treasure of intelligence to him ; and, whenever he was at a loss for any
particular trait of countenance, he had recourse to
his tablets, and there found ample reason to applaud
his former industry; for, as has before been observed, he never lost an opportunity of drawing every
remarkable countenance that he could meet with.
This he considered to be of such utility, that he always
carried a small sketch-book in his girdle, in which he
drew whatever made the most impression on his imagination; and he advised all artists to do the same.
It was his opinion that nature was the best teacher;
and for that reason he obliged his scholars to delineate
the most extraordinary as well as the most beautiful
features they could meet with, which he considered
the best means of taking good likenesses. Had he
entertained any doubt of the usefulness of this system,
the assistance he derived from it in his great work of
" The Last Supper," where he had so many different
feelings and passions to pourtray, would have been
sufficient to confirm his opinion.

This inimitable picture has been so frequently described, and so universally eulogised, that there is
little which is new to be said upon the subject, and
any description of that painting would be superfluous
after the beautiful engraving made from it by the
Chevalier Raphael Morghen. It therefore only remains to join in the general regret excited by its too
speedy decay, which has deprived the world of what
formed the glory of Da Vinci, and the wonder of the
age in which he lived. As far back as the middle of

sixteenth century, Armenini speaks of this picture as
half destroyed : if we may believe Da Vinci's friend and
scholar Lomazzo, who frequently mentions it in his
Treatise, the colours soon disappeared, so that the
outlines only remained to indicate the excellence of
the drawing. In the early part of the seventeenth
century, both Cardinal Borromeo and Padre Gattico,
who resided some time in the Dominican Convent at
Milan, agree in saying of this picture, " che del Ce-
nacolo vedeansi solo le reliquie ;" and that from its
continually mouldering away, copies had been taken
of it in all sizes by most of the celebrated artists of
that time, and which are now dispersed throughout
Italy.* In 1624, Bartolomeo Sanese, who saw both
the original and the famous copy in the Chartreuse
Convent of Pavia, by Marco Oggioni, declared that
more praise was due to the Chartreuse than the Dominicans ; as, while Leonardo's own work was so

* The following is the most authentic list of the ancient copies
still extant :—

1. In the Franciscan Convent at Milan, by Lomazzo, in 1561.

2. In St. Barnabas, a small copy by Marco Oggioni.

3. At St. Peter's, a copy by Santagostino.

4. In the Grand Monastery, by Lomazzo.

5. In the Public Library, done by order of Cardinal Borromeo.

6. In the Monastery of the Jesuits, two miles from Milan, by
Oggioni.

7. In the Grand Chartreuse at Pavia, by the same.

8. At St. Benedetto, at Mantua, by Monsignori.

9. At Lugano, by Bernardino Luino.

10. In Spain, at the Escurial, by Luino.

11. In France, at St. Germain's, painted by Luino, by order of
Francis the First.

12. At Ecoens, painter unknown.

much destroyed by age and damp as to be scarcely discernible, the copy would be the means of handing it down to the admiration of posterity. The picture became gradually so much worse, that Scannelli, who saw it in 1642, observes, that " There are but few vestiges remaining of the figures ; and the naked parts, such as heads, hands, and feet, are almost entirely annihilated." This is the only excuse the Dominicans could possibly have for cutting off the feet of our Saviour and several of the Apostles near him, in order to enlarge their entrance into the refectory. Nothing but the extreme decay of the picture itself could palliate so senseless an act; and it is most probable that it remained in this neglected state until 1726, when the painter, Bellotti, succeeded in cleaning and restoring it so well that it appeared to revive, and almost to regain its former beauty. Many writers assert that Bellotti simply repainted it on Da Vinci's outlines ; but this is denied by his contemporaries, and Padre Pino assures us that he " made the picture revive by some secret of his own, retouching with the point of his brush only those places where the colour was quite peeled off."

Notwithstanding Bellotti's labours to preserve this painting, it soon began to lose its newly acquired beauty, and to peel off and moulder away in such a manner that the Abbate Luigi Lanzi, in his celebrated work of the " Storia Pittorica dell' Italia," observes, that there were only three heads in the whole picture that could be considered as Leonardo's painting. However, it remained tolerably discernible until the Dominicans themselves were driven out of their Convent when the French army invaded Italy under Na-

poleon. The Convent was then used as a cavalry
depôt, and the refectory turned into a stable ; so that
the brutality of the soldiery soon completed what the
ignorance of the priesthood and the ravages of time
had commenced. With a spirit of destruction scarcely
to be accounted for, the troops of republican France
had no hesitation in firing at our Saviour and all the
Apostles, leaving more proofs of their skill as marks-
men than of their feelings as Christians or civilized
beings.

It is now so much destroyed that it is even a matter
of dispute whether it was originally painted in oil,
fresco, or tempera. That it was done in oil is most
probable, from it always having been said so in the
earliest engravings, and spoken of as such in contemporaneous writings, and also from its speedy decay,
there being rarely an instance of the durability of oil
painting upon walls. Many authors pretend that the
colours faded so soon from Da Vinci's having made
use of some particular varnish or chemical preparation,
as he was always considered too fond of experiments.
Had Leonardo been merely a painter, he would have
been contented with the usual methods of painting ;
but his lofty genius and love of new inventions tended
on this, as on many other occasions, to eclipse his
fame ; for, had it been otherwise, this great work
might have been spared to the present age. Much of
the destruction which this picture has suffered must
doubtless be attributed to bad restoration ; and considerable allowances should be made for the envy
of his contemporaries.

We may endeavour to trace the progress of its
decay, as the only consolation which remains to us for

such a loss; and when we consider the time in which it was executed, it must be allowed to have been one of the greatest works of art ever undertaken. Raphael's "School of Athens," is considered by some as a work of greater merit; but it should be recollected that a number of years had elapsed between the paint-ing of these two pictures, and that great progress had been made in the arts during that period. Besides, it is scarcely just to Leonardo da Vinci that Raphael should claim superiority from having profited by the improvements which his predecessor had introduced. It is a curious coincidence that the two invasions of Italy by the French should have been equally detri-mental to Da Vinci's two great works, although so many centuries intervened between them; as Monsig-nore Sabba da Castiglione, a noble Milanese, tells us in his "Ricordi," that "he saw the bowmen of Gas-cony make use of Da Vinci's model for the colossal statue of Francesco Sforza as a target," and many noble Milanese of the present day could tell us in their "ricordi," that they saw the troops of republican France make a somewhat similar use of his magnificent picture of "The Last Supper."

In 1497, Ludovico's wife, Beatrice of Este, died after a short illness, and the Duke honoured her me-mory, according to Corio, with a "stupendissime ossequie." From several notes in his tablets we find that these were directed by Leonardo, which affords an additional proof of his patron's confidence.

It was about this time that he became acquainted with Andrea Salaj'no, whom he received into his stu-dio, and soon admitted to his intimate friendship. He had the greatest regard for this young man, and took great pleasure in teaching him every thing relating to painting; in which he acquired such proficiency, that some of his works in Milan have been falsely attributed to Leonardo. The probability is, that some of them were corrected by him, or had the advantage of receiving his finishing touches. Salaj'no was so gratefully attached to his master, that he never quitted him from that period, and was the constant companion and sharer of his fortunes.

Da Vinci's principal occupation during this year was the navigation of the Adda, between Brizzio and Frezzo. This was a most difficult undertaking, from the rapidity of the stream, and the numerous shoals which impeded its progress, and obliged him to excavate a new canal, and form strong supports to prevent the banks from falling in. From different circumstances we may believe that he formed plans to overcome all these difficulties, though it does not appear that they were carried into effect at that period, as the political troubles which embarrassed his patron obliged him to put a sudden termination to many of the works of art which he had previously undertaken.

It is not known that Leonardo painted any thing of consequence subsequent to his grand work of " The Last Supper," before the misfortunes of the house of Sforza obliged him to return to his own country, except another portrait of the beautiful Cecilia Gallerani, on wood, which is at present in the possession of the Palavicini family at San Calocero.

The greatest mortification to Leonardo was his being obliged to abandon all idea of finishing the equestrian statue of Francesco Sforza, which was to have been cast in bronze, and had already occupied

him so many years. His mould was prepared, and
nothing was wanting but the metal, which the Duke
was no longer able to furnish, as, according to Da
Vinci's own calculation, it would have taken 200,000
pounds weight of bronze. In vain did Leonardo solicit
his friends to use their utmost influence with the
Duke; in vain did the poets of the court endeavour
to flatter him into acquiescence with Da Vinci's
wishes; Ludovico no longer had it in his power to
expend money on the fine arts, but was obliged to
employ the little that remained in his own defence.

Da Vinci's situation must now have been extremely
unpleasant, as it appears from a fragment of one of his
own letters, that the Duke owed him more than two
years' salary. He must have been in great pecuniary
embarrassment before his pride would have permitted
him to have written "that he was no longer able to
continue his works at his own expense, as he had not
the means either of paying his workmen or purchasing
his materials." It must have been a most bitter dis-
appointment to him to have found his time so thrown
away, as he could no longer entertain any hope of
making his cast of this statue, on which he had bestowed so much labour, and from which he had expected to have derived so much fame. His enemies
assert that his design was too grand and speculative
to have been ever carried into effect; but great allowances should be made for the envy excited by his
talents and success at the court of Milan.

It appears, however, from several memoranda in his
own hand-writing, that Leonardo himself not only
considered it possible, but had made his calculations
with the greatest nicety, and would have, no doubt,

succeeded in his undertaking, had not the political events of the times put it entirely out of his power.

In the following year, 1495, the Duke gave Leonardo a proof of his friendship and generosity, by making him a present of a small estate near the Porta Vercellina, with full power to bequeath it to whom he pleased, or to dispose of it in any way he thought proper.*   Whether this land was given as a compensation for the arrears that were justly his due, or as a gift for services received by the state, is immaterial ; most probably the Duke wished to avert as much as possible the want and misery to which he feared Da Vinci would be exposed in the event of his own ruin, as he had been exclusively employed for the benefit of the house of Sforza and the government of Milan.   It is a proof, however, of Il Moro's goodness of heart, that he could remember the wants of his friends when pursued on all sides by his enemies.   Shortly after he was forced to fly from the city.

The flight of his patron, and the subsequent change in the government of Milan, must have caused the greatest regret to Da Vinci and his friends, who had equal reason to lament his fate as a prince and an in-

---

* This gift is registered in the public office at Milan as follows :—

" 1429, 26 Aprilis, Ludovicus Maria Sfortia, dux Mediolani, dono dedit D. Leonardo Quintio (*sic*) Florentio, pictori celeberrimo, pert. n. 16 soli seu fundi ejus vinae quam ab Abate seu Monasterio S. Victoris in suburbano portæ Vercellinæ proxime acquisierat, ut in eo spatio soli pro ejus arbitrio ædificare, colere hortos, et quicquid ei vel posteris ejus, vel quibus dederit ut supra, libuerit, facere et disponere possit."—Copied verbatim from the Register.

dividual, as they were all obliged to him for the means
of continuing their studies and exercising their talents.
He had been their patron and friend; and although his
enemies accuse him of having encouraged the fine arts
solely from ostentation, the greatest praise is due to
him for the manner in which he promoted general
knowledge. His worth must have also been more
appreciated by his literary friends when brought into
comparison with their new masters; for Louis the
Twelfth, after he had made his grand entry into Milan,
thought of nothing but fêtes and entertainments during
the time he remained there; and the French in general
were extremely indifferent to the progress of literature
and the arts. They destroyed a magnificent building
which Leonardo had designed for Galeazzo da San
Severino, and wantonly broke up his model for the
equestrian statue, both of which must have caused him
great mortification.

Finding his talents neglected, himself unrewarded,
and his works no longer esteemed, without any immediate
diate prospect of his former patron's re-establishment
in Milan, Leonardo determined to leave a city where
his finances were so much reduced, and his situation
so unpleasantly altered. It appears, however, that he
delayed his departure until the year 1500, and that he
waited the issue of Il Moro's return to Milan at the
request of his faithless subjects, when they revolted
against the French. Hoping to maintain himself by
force, the ex-Duke raised a body of Swiss mercenaries,
who, instead of fighting in his defence, basely sold
him to his enemies, by whom he was taken in disguise
with his brother the Cardinal Ascanio, and several of
his followers. Il Moro was imprisoned in the castle of

Loches, in France, where he died of a broken heart at the unhappy issue of all his wild dreams of ambition, after ten years' confinement.

During the uncertainty of this revolution, while awaiting the result of his patron's last struggle for power, Da Vinci remained at Vaprio,* to be out of the way of the cabals and disturbances of the capital. This would have given him an opportunity of studying the source of the Adda, which had always been a favourite object of his researches. Or perhaps he lingered behind in hopes of seeing Milan again restored to tranquillity, and the love for the arts revived in a place where he had so highly distinguished himself. He must also have been extremely unwilling to lose the fruits of his long services to this state, as he considered himself attached to the court of Milan, whatever sovereign might be at the head of that government. But, perceiving at length that the French thought of nothing but their amusements, he made up his mind to return to his own country; and shortly after, accompanied by his friends Salaj'no and Luca Paciolo, set out for Florence, where he resolved to take up his residence, and hoped to find employment.

In the mean time the government of Florence had passed into other hands, and had undergone an almost

---

* The Melzi Villa, at Vaprio, is half-way betwwen Milan and Bergamo, on the canal of the Martesana, which was the work of Leonardo, and which, as well from its utility as from the difficulties he surmounted in its execution, would have been sufficient to immortalize his memory. The situation was extremely pleasant, and this place was a great favourite with Da Vinci, who frequently retired there.

entire change.   Disgusted with the arrogance and
imbecility of Pietro dei Medici's conduct, his fellow-
citizens had revolted from his sway, and banished him
and his whole family, declaring them enemies to the
state.   They had elected Pietro Soderini, one of their
principal citizens, as their Lord, with the title of
"Gonfaloniere Perpetuo," and the city was now en-
joying more tranquillity than it had experienced since
the death of Lorenzo the Magnificent.   The immense
wealth produced by their extensive commerce enabled
the Florentines to cultivate the fine arts, and adorn
their city with public buildings, notwithstanding the
miseries and disturbances occasioned by the perpetual
struggles of contending parties to obtain a preponder-
ance in the government of the state.   Their patriotism
and public spirit overcame every difficulty, and the
pride of all was interested in enriching their country
with works of art, and in giving employment to the
first artists of the age.

Leonardo da Vinci was received with every distinction by the Gonfaloniere, who immediately enrolled
him in the list of those artists who were employed by
the government, and assigned him a sufficient pension
to provide for his subsistence, which enabled him to
form a tolerably comfortable establishment, with his
friend Paciolo and his scholar Salaj'no. On the subject
of this pension, Vasari relates the following anecdote.

" Leonardo was very high-minded, and extremely
generous in all his actions. It is said that, going one
day to the bank for the monthly provision that he was
accustomed to receive from Pietro Soderini, the
cashier wanted to give him some bundles of halfpence,

which he refused, saying, I am not a halfpenny painter."*

It is a great pity that Da Vinci allowed his pride to have so much ascendency over his better judgment. His irritable sensibility was his greatest enemy through life, and was the occasion of his losing many friends, who had both the power and inclination to assist him. This prevailing foible was also extremely detrimental to his fame in his profession, as it frequently blinded him to the difficulties of executing the vast conceptions of his all-comprehensive mind. His brilliant imagination made him suppose that every thing must give way to his abilities, and led him into errors which have deprived posterity of some of his best works. His ideas were too gigantic for the age in which he lived, and it would have been much better for his reputation as a painter if he had been a less universally accomplished man.

After his return to Florence, he pursued his studies with unremitting assiduity, and diligently worked at his profession, which he was the more obliged to attend to from no longer having the advantage of so good a salary as he had enjoyed at Milan. Instead of the luxuries and extravagances of Il Moro's splendid court, he had now to accommodate himself to the more prudent restrictions of a republic, whose slmptuary laws were enacted in a spirit of economy quite different to what he had seen at Milan.

---

* " Io non sono un dipintore per quatrini." The quatrino is translated in the text as a halfpenny, to make it the more intelligible ; its real value is the fifth part of a grazia, which is the eighth of a franc, valued at 6½d. English.

d

The first work of consequence in which he was engaged, was an altar-piece for the church of the
" Annunziata." Unfortunately, however, he only
formed the design of this picture, which is generally
called the Cartoon of Santa Anna, which was so ex-
quisitely finished, that Vasari says, " not only all the
artists, but the whole city, men and women, young
and old, flocked to see it in such crowds, that for two
days it had almost the appearance of a public festival."
The same author describes the artist's having successfully expressed in the countenance of the Virgin Mary
" all the grace which simplicity and beauty could possibly give to the mother of Christ, anxious to show the
modesty, humility, and thankfulness, which she might
be supposed to feel in contemplating the beauty of
her child, which she is supporting in her lap ; while
she is looking down at St. John, a little boy playing
with a kid, encouraged by the smiles of Santa Anna,
who is delighted to see her terrestrial progeny thus
become almost celestial." " A consideration," he
further observes, " truly worthy of Leonardo's talents
and genius." This picture was carried to France in
the time of Francis the First ; but it must have found
its way back to Italy, as it belonged to Aurelio Luino,
when Lomazzo wrote his Treatise on Painting.

About this time Da Vinci applied himself more particularly to portraits, and painted two of the most
celebrated beauties of Florence ; the Lady Ginevra,
wife of Amerigo Benci, which, according to Vasari,
was " una cosa bellissima," and the Madonna Lisa, wife
of Francesco del Giocondo, which all the artists and
writers of that period considered as the perfection of
portrait-painting. Vasari describes this picture in so

very minute and lively a manner, that it is impossible to give a more accurate description of it, than by making use of his own words, written on the spot shortly after it was finished: " In this head the beholder may observe how nearly it is possible for art to approach nature. The eyes have the lustre and expression of life. The nose, and more particularly the mouth, have more the appearance of real flesh and blood than painting, from the beautiful contrast of the vermillion of the lips with the clear red and white of the complexion. Whoever attentively looks at the throat, can almost see the beating of the pulse. As the Madonna Lisa was a very beautiful woman, Leonardo studied all possible means of making her picture surpass every thing that had been then seen of the sort. He was in the habit of having music, singing, and all kinds of buffoonery to make her laugh and remove the air of melancholy so frequently to be observed in portrait-painting; which produced so pleasing an effect in this picture, that it gave to the canvass an almost superhuman expression, and the only wonder seemed to be that it was not alive."

Francis the First bought this picture for his collection at Fontainbleau, and paid 4000 gold crowns to the family for whom it was painted, a sum that would be equal to 45,000 francs in the present day. It is now in the Louvre, and is considered one of the finest specimens of Leonardo's painting extant; it is called " La belle Joconde," and there is a landscape in the back-ground.

After remaining two years at Florence, Da Vinci travelled over the greater part of Italy, and made notes and drawings of whatever he found instructive

and amusing. It would have been highly interesting
to have had an opportunity of collecting the remarks
of a traveller so perfectly capable of describing whatever he saw, and who united in himself the different
qualifications of a painter, mechanic, and architect,
with the philosophical feelings of a liberal-minded
man. He must have visited the whole of Romagna, as
we find from his notes he was at Urbino on the 30th
July, 1502, where he designed the fortress. He went
to Pesaro, Rinucci, and Cesena, where he remarks
" the picturesque manner in which the vines were sus-
pended in festoons." It would have been difficult to
have assigned a reason for his having consumed his
time and money in travelling, if it were not sufficiently
explained by the fact of the Duca Valentino's having
appointed him his surveyor and engineer general, as
that would have obliged him to visit all the strong
places, of which the Duke had usurped the dominion
as Gonfaloniere or Captain-General of the ecclesias-
tical army. The immoderate ambition of the house of
Borgia was, in this instance, of material service to
Leonardo, enabling him to see more of his country
than he had hitherto done, without any expense to
himself; as it is well known that, whatever were Valentino's vices, he was, either from policy or ostentation,
liberal even to excess to those who were in his service.
Pope Alexander the Sixth died 18th August, 1503,
in the seventy-first year of his age, a victim, it is supposed, to his own treacherous intrigues, as he is said
to have taken a goblet of poisoned wine which he had
prepared for one of his guests. This circumstance
destroyed all the brilliant projects of the house of
Borgia, and occasioned the sudden downfall of Valentino and his dependents. He was succeeded by Julius

the Second, whose wisdom and integrity partly in-
demnified Christendom for the profligate enormities
by which his predecessor had disgraced the pontificate.
The Pope's death also speedily terminated Da Vinci's
commission, as in 1503 we find him returned to Florence, and engaged to paint one side of the council-
hall in the Palazzo Vecchio, by the desire of the Gonfaloniere Pietro Soderini.

This was the origin of all the jealousies and disputes
between Leonardo da Vinci and Michael Angelo Buonarroti, who had also been employed to make designs
for the same purpose; and hence arose a rivalry between these two great men which caused them to
exert their utmost abilities in the cartoons they respec-
tively executed. As these paintings were intended as
a sort of national monument, it was necessary to select
some trait in the Florentine history, which might at
once serve to commemorate the glory of the republic
and the fame of the painter. From a long memorandum in Leonardo's handwriting, we find that he had
chosen for his subject the defeat of Nicolo Picinino,
the Milanese General, near Anghiari, in Tuscany, and
that he had collected every circumstance of this battle,
either real or fictitious, in order to delineate it properly. We can easily perceive from his remarks the
labour he must have bestowed on collecting materials
for this picture, which, it is much to be regretted, was
never executed, as Vasari relates that having tried his
preparations on the wall, for painting it in oil, he
found it did not succeed, and therefore abandoned the
undertaking altogether.* Here is another instance of

* The memorandum for this picture is given in Brown's Life
(Appendix, No. III.), from Leonardo's manuscript. It is curious

his versatility of talent interfering with his fame) as a painter; for, had he been entirely ignorant of chemistry, he would necessarily have been obliged to content himself with the ordinary rules of fresco painting, and he might again have left a work that would have immortalized his name.

As these cartoons no longer exist, a description of them may prove interesting. Vasari tells us that Leonardo represented a combat of horsemen fighting for a standard, which group was only intended as a part of the historical design just alluded to. It was so wonderfully executed, that the horses themselves seemed agitated with the same fury as their riders, and were fighting as hard with their teeth as their riders with their swords, to obtain possession of the contested flag. " Neither is it possible," continues Vasari, " to describe Leonardo's designs, in the soldiers' dresses so beautifully varied, as well as in the incredible skill he showed in the forms and attitudes of the horses, as no other artist could delineate the muscles and actions of the horse with sueh uncommon beauty and fidelity." *   Michael Angelo's cartoon represented a troop of soldiers suddenly called to arms when bathing, and the scene of his picture was the siege of Pisa by the Florentines, and has been so fully described by Mr. Duppa in his Life of that great artist, that it need not be here repeated.   Both these cartoons were shown

to observe the minute details he entered into in his compositions, and with what extreme accuracy he studied to increase the interest of his historical performances.

* One part of Leonardo's cartoon was engraved by Marc Antonio, the other by Agostino Veneziano. The former is called " Les grimpeurs," and both are exceedingly rare.

in the Medici palace until the death of the Duke
Giuliano, when they disappeared without any person
being able to account for it. Vasari says that Michael
Angelo's was torn in pieces, and that in his time there
was a small piece, remaining in the hands of a dillet-
tante at Mantua. It may be supposed in what esteem
they must have been held, when their fame was sufficient to induce Raphael to come to Florence for the
sole purpose of studying them. He was so much surprised and delighted at their freedom of manner and
boldness of execution, that from that moment he is
said to have resolved to abandon the stiffness and poverty of his master Pietro Perugino's style.

During his stay in Tuscany, Leonardo renewed his
former friendship with Giovan Francesco Rustici,*
who had been his fellow-student with Andrea Varocchio when they were both young men. Rustici was
a man of good family, and more an artist from inclination than necessity. He had the good taste to listen
to Da Vinci's criticism, to whom he was particularly
attached; and was also well acquainted with the worth
of his observations. He was esteemed a good sculptor and architect by his contemporaries, as well as by
his friend Leonardo; and the three statues which he
cast in bronze for the baptistery at Florence, remain
to this day memorials of his fame.

In 1504 Leonardo da Vinci lost his father, with
whom he had always continued on the most affectionate

* Giovan Francesco Rustici was a man of a very extraordinary
turn of mind; he became the founder of a society or club called
the Pajuolo, of which the account, given by Vasari, is very illus-
trative of the manners of the times.

terms. Whatever might have been his birth, he had
made a point of keeping up a constant correspondence
and perfectly good understanding with his family. It
appears that soon after the Signore Pietro's death, he
placed a considerable sum of money at interest with
the chamberlain of Santa Maria Nuova, as there are
several memoranda among his papers of his having
received small payments at different times from this
person, and he afterwards disposed of this particular
property in his will. From this we may suppose that
some of his works had been very liberally rewarded,
as this money could only have been acquired by his
own exertions. It is Ammoretti's opinion that he
visited France in 1506, but there is not sufficient proof
of his having undertaken that journey, in the several
memoranda on which this gentleman hazards his
assertion; for they might have as easily referred to
his subsequent residence in that country, although he
certainly considered himself in the service of the King
of France as sovereign of Milan. In whatever way
he employed the intermediate time, it is certain that
Leonardo was again in Lombardy in 1507, as there is
the following memorandum in his own handwriting:
" Canonica di Vaprio, a dì 5 Luglio 1507, cara mia
diletta Madre et mia Sorella et mia Cognata avvissovi
come sono sano per la grazia di Dio," &c.; which
sufficiently proves the fact of his having been staying
at that time with his friends the Melzi. That he was
frequently in the habit of residing with them, not only
at their house at Canonica, but also at their palace at
Vaprio, there remains a proof as glorious to the artist's
feelings as to his generous patrons, in the picture of
the Madonna and Child which he painted on the wall

of his apartment in their palace. The head of the Madonna is six palms in height, and that of the Child four. This painting suffered considerably in 1796, by some soldiers having made a fire close to the wall on which it is executed; but the faces are still in tolerable preservation.

In 1507 Louis the Twelfth of France, finding himself continually disturbed in the possession of his Lombard dominions by the Venetians and the States of the Church, joined the famous league of Cambray, that he might be at more liberty to invade Italy with a sufficient force to establish his affairs on a firmer basis of political security. At Agnadello, near the Adda, the King gained a complete victory over the Venetians, and returned to Milan to celebrate his triumphs and revive the drooping spirits of its inhabitants by the presence of his splendid court. These fêtes and entertainments must have again called forth Leonardo's exertions, for they are described with great pomp by Arluno, in a manuscript now in the Ambrosian Library, who talks of the triumphal arches and paintings executed by the first masters in honour of the occasion. Although he does not mention Leonardo da Vinci's name, he evidently alludes to him by his making use of the phrase "pitture mollissime," which that author was accustomed to apply to him alone. Besides which, it is well known that he was in great favour with his Majesty at that time, as he appointed him painter to the court of France, and gave him twelve ounces of water from the canal of the Martesana, which was a sort of right of property extremely valuable to its possessor. As far as this gift can be at present understood, it appears that he was entitled

to as much water as could be drawn off by a tunnel
that measured one foot in diameter, which is equal to
twelve ounces, and that he had the right of applying
this to whatever purpose he pleased.   To an engineer
of his talents this was of the greatest value, as he
might have either applied it to hydraulical purposes,
or sold it to the proprietors of the neighbouring lands
to enrich the cultivation of their soil by its irrigations.
By his letters from Florence it would appear that he
intended making the former use of it, but the latter
would also have yielded him a handsome revenue.   It
is not likely that he ever realized this property, but he
showed that he considered it belonged to him, by dis-
posing of it in his will.   While in attendance on the
French court at Milan, he painted the portrait of
Gian Jacopo Triulzio, which is mentioned by Lomazzo,
and is now in the Public Gallery at Dresden.

  The death of his uncle, Messer Francesco da Vinci,
a share in whose inheritance his brothers contested
with him, on the ground of his illegitimacy, determined
him to go to Florence to settle the dispute.   It is not
known how the affair was determined between them,
but we may be allowed to conjecture that it must have
been in an amicable manner, from the circumstance of
his leaving his property in and near Florence to be
equally divided between his brothers at his death.   In
1512 he returned to Milan, where he principally employed himself in hydraulical researches, in order to
perfect the canal by which he had brought the Adda
to the walls of the city.   But he was again destined to
be interrupted in his professional occupations ; for he
had scarcely time to see his friends, and get settled in
his habitation, before the new government of Milan

was broken up, and the tranquillity of Lombardy so much destroyed, that he was again obliged to seek refuge in a more peaceful quarter.

The Princes of Italy, jealous of the presence of a foreign army, whose power might become inimical to their interests, concluded a league with the Emperor to replace the house of Sforza on the throne of Lombardy. In a short time Maximilian, the eldest son of Il Moro, returned in triumph to take undisputed possession of his paternal inheritance, escorted by the same Swiss mercenaries who had so shortly before betrayed his father. He was received with acclamations and rejoicings by the inhabitants of Milan. Leonardo himself, although belonging, as he conceived, to the court of France, was sufficiently attached to the remembrance of his old patron, to paint two portraits of the young Duke Maximilian, one of which is now in the Gallery of Milan, and the other in the private collection of the Melzi family. But the situation of Milan, and the disturbed state of politics in Italy, were so extremely detrimental to Da Vinci's projects, that he was almost unable to procure a subsistence by his profession. Between the two governments he had already lost what he considered as a provision for his old age, as he was now more than sixty, and no longer possessed that buoyant feeling and ardent disposition that carried him through every thing in youth. It was quite in vain for Leonardo, or any of his followers and companions in the Academy, to think of remaining in a place where nothing was to be expected but tumults and revenge. Literature and the fine arts are nurtured by peace and tranquillity alone ; where these cease to exist, the artist who

desires to increase his reputation had better depart
also. Accordingly, we find by the following memorandum, that Leonardo at last set out for Rome,
accompanied by his principal friends and scholars:
" Partii da Milano per Roma ad dì 24 di Settembre
1514, con Giovanni, Francesco Melzi, Salaj, Lorenzo
ed il Fanfoia." *

Leonardo arrived in safety at Florence, where he
found the power of the house of Medici restored by
the election of the Cardinal Giovanni to the pontificate,
under the name of Leo the Tenth, after the decease
of Julius the Second. The Pope's brother, Giuliano
de' Medici received him into his household and took
him to Rome. Every individual possessed of either
talents or reputation was then hastening to that capital
to recommend himself to the notice of Leo the Tenth;
a pontiff whose name must ever be respected in the
annals of literature and the arts, and whose princely
liberality, by completing the restoration of learning,
made Rome once more mistress of the civilized world.

Although advanced in years, and the ardour of feeling considerably abated by the experience which can
only be acquired from a knowledge of the world and
its disappointments, Da Vinci yet hoped to distinguish
himself amongst those who contended for the Pope's
favour.

On his arrival he was well received by Leo, both
from the high reputation he enjoyed, and the circumstance of his being presented to the Pontiff by his brother

* Probably this Giovanni means " il Beltraffio," but there is
no mention of any person called Fanfoia, unless it is a mistake
for Fojano, who is frequently spoken of by Lomazzo and others
in their manuscripts.

Giuliano, whose favour da Vinci had completely
gained. But his talents excited the envy of all those
who surrounded his Holiness's person and had already
secured his confidence, as they considered his approach as a sort of invasion of what they had appropriated to themselves as a right: so seldom can men
of genius bear with any sort of competition. No one
was more free from this unworthy feeling of envy than
Leonardo himself; no one more anxious to do ample
justice to the merits of others; but, most deservedly,
accustomed to hold the first place at Milan, and conscious that many of the improvements in the arts
which he now saw brought into use, were owing to
his own inventions and to the improvements which he
himself had introduced, he could not avoid feeling
most acutely that he no longer possessed the same
superiority over others which he had done in his
youth. If he had given himself time to think, he would
have been consoled by the reflection that this was the
natural consequence of the progress of the arts, to
which he, more than any other person, had eminently
contributed. Instead of feeling mortified at the practice of the theory which he himself had first propa-
gated, he ought to have rejoiced at its having met
with the success which he had originally contemplated.
But his bodily health was no longer equal to the
energy of his mind, and his increasing infirmities made
him more than usually irritable, for he had naturally
too much pride to indulge any feelings of vanity.

Under these circumstances it was not to be expected
that Da Vinci could have felt himself happily situated
at Rome. Harassed by disappointments, his genius
was overcast by the praises he heard on all sides

bestowed on others, whom he could not have considered in any way superior to himself. But they enjoyed a greater share of his Holiness's favour, and
kept Leonardo in the back-ground by persuading the
Pope that he embraced too many branches of science
to be able to succeed in any, and that he was become
much too speculative in his ideas to execute any work
of importance. By these and similar calumnies, unworthy their own fame, and prompted solely by jea-
lousy, they contrived to keep Da Vinci without any
employment worthy of his talents.

Of all the celebrated persons who at that time ornamented the court of Rome, Raffaelle enjoyed the
greatest share of the Pope's confidence and esteem,
although he was more considerably indebted to his
predecessor Pope Julius the Second. That Pontiff
first brought him into notice at the recommendation
of his kinsman, Bramante da Urbino, who was then in
his service, and employed him to paint a suite of
rooms in the Vatican. He executed this commission
with such extraordinary taste and skill, that the frescoes he then painted are generally considered superior
to any of his subsequent productions under the reign
of Leo the Tenth.

The great Michael Angelo, who was also at Rome
at that period, had not the good fortune to be so much
distinguished by Leo as he had been by Julius, who
was his friend and patron; and it ought to be observed, in justice to the latter, that many of the great
works, the whole praise of which has been unthink-
ingly bestowed on Leo, more properly belonged to
his predecessor, he having originally undertaken them,
though Leo had the liberality and generosity to carry

them into effect. If Leonardo da Vinci had enjoyed
the advantage of the protection of Julius the Second,
he would, no doubt, have been in a much better situation; and had he employed that time in his service
which he lost during the disturbances at Milan, he
would not only have been at the head of his profession
as an artist, but his knowledge of military tactics, and
his talents as an engineer, would have made him an
invaluable acquisition to that warlike Pontiff.

The reign of Leo the Tenth forms so striking an
era in Italian literature, that one is too apt to confound him personally with the age in which he lived.
Without at all wishing to deteriorate the good qualities
which this magnificent Pontiff undoubtedly possessed,
it appears from the history of those times, that the age
contributed more to his elevation, than he did individually to the advancement of learning. Had Julius
lived a few years longer, we should have talked of the
Julian age of Rome, instead of " the golden days of
Leo," and the advantages to mankind would have
been much the same. The ruling principle of Leo's
policy was the aggrandisement of the house of Medici;
and by simply following the taste of the age, and acting up to the spirit of the times, he could most easily
attain his object, while he gratified his own taste for
splendour by becoming the liberal patron of men of
letters. It is easy to be generous, even to profusion,
of what does not belong to us; and few of St. Peter's
representatives have ever made a freer use of his patri-
mony. Circumstances made Leo what he was, and
unless he had abandoned the pontificate altogether
he must have been talked and flattered into virtues
which he might not have otherwise possessed. It is

certainly no proof of his discernment or good taste,
that he either could not or did not appreciate the
talents of Leonardo da Vinci sufficiently to fix him
near his person; while it is well known that he neglected those of Michael Angelo Buonarroti.

Leonardo, however, during his short stay in Rome
was not altogether unemployed, as he painted a picture for Messer Baldassare da Pescia, the Pope's da-
tario (almoner), who seemed to have more feeling for
his merits than his master. This picture was painted
on wood, and represented a Holy Family, consisting
of the Virgin and Child, with St. Joseph and St. John
behind, in which group was a portrait of a young lady
in full length, of singular beauty and noble features.
De Pagave, in speaking of this picture, observes that,
" although the Vincian style is perfectly discernible, it
is evident that he had imitated Raffaelle in this composition ;" and for this reason he probably chose to
distinguish it by the monogram of his own name, that
it might not be taken for the work of any other artist.
The beautiful lady whose portrait he introduced in
this picture, is supposed to be the Pope's sister-in-law,
as it is very natural that Leonardo should have paid
this compliment to his patron's wife, Giuliano de' Medici having just married Filiberta of Savoy.   Whoever
the lady might have been, the picture was so wonderfully executed that it attracted the Pope's attention,
and occasioned him to employ Da Vinci, old as he was,
in preference to Raffaelle and Michael Angelo, in the
execution of a work which afterwards became the
cause of his disgrace and of his departure from Rome.
Vasari relates the story, that Leonardo, with his usual
love of experiments, began to distil different herbs

and oils to make a particular kind of varnish, and that some ill-natured persons told this to the Pope, who exclaimed, " Oh ! this man will never do any thing, for he begins to think of the end of his work before the commencement." This hasty remark was immediately repeated to Leonardo, who, already disgusted with his Holiness for having sent for Michael Angelo to Rome, with whom he was on bad terms, determined on leaving it.

It is not to be wondered at, that so high-minded a man as Leonardo should have been offended at such an observation. Conscious of his own merits, and indignant at the neglect with which he had been treated during his residence at the papal court, he could not do otherwise than resolve to quit a place where he had met with so many vexations, and seek another patron in spite of his age and infirmities. There is nothing to be collected, either from his notes or the manuscripts in the Ambrosian Library, to prove that he undertook any thing more of consequence at Rome, except some improvements he introduced in the mint for purifying and embellishing the Roman coin. Before his misunderstanding with the Pope, he had most likely painted the fresco of the Virgin on the walls of St. Onofrio, of which nothing now remains ; as well as several other pictures for various individuals, who still cherished his name, and were anxious to possess some specimen of his abilities.

It was most unworthy of Leo's character, as the great Mæcenas of the whole Christian world, to have treated Leonardo da Vinci with so little consideration. If for no other reasons but his former works, long experience, and great reputation, he should have received

him with kindness. The extreme amiability of his
manners towards all might have at least blunted the
shafts of envy and ill-nature. That he was himself
superior to such meanness, he had given a proof in the
last picture he painted, where he had, in a great measure, adopted the ease of Raffaelle's style, in addition
to the exquisite softness and minute finishing of his
own. It was no small compliment to Raffaelle that
Leonardo, even in his old age, should have conde-
scended to imitate him ; for in such a man it was condescension to alter his style in imitation of any one.
Although it would be impossible to deny that Raffaelle
excelled Da Vinci in painting nearly as much as
Michael Angelo did in sculpture, still it must be generally allowed, that, if they were the greater artists, he
was the greater man, without derogating from the high
character of either. When we consider the state in
which Leonardo da Vinci found the arts when he first
engaged in painting as a profession, the improvements
which he introduced, the scholars whom he educated,
and the prejudices which he annihilated, we are all
lost in admiration of his various merits. Even Michael
Angelo and Raffaelle are obliged to him for a part
of their glory; because they first became the great
men they were from studying his works. Raffaelle
borrowed from him that almost divine grace, which
Leonardo so well knew how to impart to the countenances he painted; Michael Angelo took from him
that daring style of drawing by which he astonished
mankind; and if afterwards both surpassed him, they
were nevertheless infinitely indebted to the advantages
they derived from his original inventions. Yet, such
is the ungrateful reward of talent in all times, this man

was obliged to expatriate himself when more than seventy years of age!

The politics of Italy were now again becoming embroiled. King Louis the Twelfth of France died on the first day of the year 1515, and he was succeeded by Francis the First. It was not to be supposed that a young King of only twenty-two years of age would feel inclined to submit quietly to the loss of his Italian dominions, particularly as he had assumed the title of Duke of Milan on his accession to the throne, both in right of his predecessor and of the Emperor's concession of that duchy at the league of Cambray. Having concluded an advantageous peace with the King of England and the Archduke of Austria, afterwards Charles V., the young monarch advanced towards Italy, determined to make light of every difficulty. His successes induced Leo to incline towards an accommodation. Francis was already in possession of Pavia; and his armies were proceeding with rapid strides to reconquer the whole of Lombardy.

These political events no sooner became public than Leonardo da Vinci resolved to profit by the successes of his former patrons, the French, in whose service he still considered himself. He therefore set out for Pavia, where he was received by Francis with every mark of friendship. He soon became a great favourite with his Majesty, who delighted in his society and conversation; and Da Vinci's spirits began to revive at again finding himself in a situation where all his excellent qualities were duly appreciated. He felt himself of the same consequence he had formerly been; and presiding over the revels and entertainments of a magnificent court, he exerted his utmost

taste and skill to please his chivalrous patron and his
nobles.

It is supposed that the Lion, spoken of by Lomazzo,
was contrived by Leonardo on this occasion to increase
the pomp of some of the fêtes given in honour of the
King's successes. This piece of mechanism was so
admirably contrived, that the lion walked of itself up
to the King's throne, and threw open its body, which
was filled with "fleurs de lis," in compliment to his
Majesty. This pageant is frequently mentioned by
the writers of that period, when it was, no doubt,
considered as a most wonderful invention.

Both the Pope and the King of France were extremely desirous of an interview, and Bologna was
fixed upon as the place where the congress should be
held. The King came attended with very little pomp,
and only a small part of his brilliant court, but among
them was Leonardo da Vinci,* who must have been
highly gratified in being able to show himself to the
Pope's followers as the friend and favourite of a
powerful monarch, after having been almost compelled
to quit Rome. To the young King his experience
was doubtless of the greatest use in treating with so
wary a politician as Leo; and his general knowledge
of Italy, both in politics and literature, must have
increased his favour with Francis, to whose interest he
was now most firmly attached, and from that time

* Among Leonardo's papers was found a design for the portrait of Signore Artus, under which is written, in his own hand-
writing, "Ritratto di M. Artus, Maestro di Camera del Rè Francesco primo, nella Giunta con Papa Leon decimo," which fully
proves that Da Vinci was present on that occasion.

Leonardo considered himself as belonging to the French court. Conscious of his own deserts, Leonardo da Vinci felt as an insult what was merely the effect of an envious cabal; but his sensitive mind was so deeply wounded, that he determined to abandon his country for ever, and establish himself at the court of France for the rest of his days. If his pride could have submitted to prove his superior merit by his works, instead of showing that he was offended by leaving the court of Rome, there is every probability that he must have triumphed over his enemies and regained the Pontiff's favour. But most likely he considered himself too old to begin the struggle anew, and he was perhaps too proud to submit to a competition for fame in a country where he had for so many years held the first place, and which was so much indebted to his exertions for many of the advantages which she possessed in the fine arts. Another reason that must have naturally influenced him at his time of life, was the instability of the Italian courts, the disadvantages of which he had sufficiently experienced in the down-fall of the house of Sforza, and the continual changes of the government of Milan. By these circumstances he had lost all the fruits of his long services to that state during the best part of his life; and even his reputation had considerably suffered by it, in the destruction of his works. The equestrian statue of Francesco Sforza, which he was to have cast in bronze, and by which he hoped to have established his fame as a sculptor, never proceeded any further than the model, and even that was destroyed by the brutality of the soldiery. The evils of war and the miseries of civil dissension had dispersed his friends and scholars, and nothing remained of the Academy which he had founded, but the effects which it produced on the arts in laying a foundation for the improvement of painting, by which all subsequent artists have more or less benefited. The friends of his brighter days were all either dead or no longer able to struggle against the misfortunes which they had met with from the unsettled state of their country; so that it was not to be wondered at that Da Vinci should have preferred sheltering himself under the protection of a powerful monarch who promised to provide most generously for the rest of his life, to the precarious subsistence which Italy could afford him.

Previous to his departure from Milan, the King tried every means in his power to remove the painting of "The Last Supper," in order to send it to France. Every thing was done to deprive Milan of this magnificent work which she has so badly taken care of; but it was found impracticable, although Francis would have spared no expense to have succeeded in his designs, and Leonardo did all in his power to gratify his new patron. However, all their efforts were ineffectual, and, as Vasari says, " the picture having been done immediately on the wall, his Majesty was obliged to depart with his wish ungratified, and leave the painting to the Milanese." *

About the end of January 1516 Leonardo accompanied Francis the First to Paris, as painter to the court of France, with an annual salary of 700 crowns, and a liberal provision for all his wants; where he met with a reception equal to his merits. The King

* An excellent copy of the Last Supper was purchased in Italy by Sir Thomas Lawrence, and is now at the Royal Academy.

treated him with distinguished favour, and the courtiers vied with each other in following his Majesty's example.

From the time of his arrival in France, his health began to deteriorate, so much so, that he was incapable of applying himself to any thing of consequence. It is known from the direction of a letter found among his papers, " A Monsieur Lyonard Peintre, par Amboise," that he must have been at that place ; as also from the circumstance of his will being dated from thence, in which he speaks of the furniture and valuables he possessed at " Du Cloux," about a mile from Amboise, where he most likely resided.

It does not appear probable that he painted any thing in France, as Vasari tells us that the King himself could not prevail on him to finish his cartoon of Santa Anna, which he had brought from Italy, and which was afterwards painted by some of his scholars on his outlines. It is also most likely that Leonardo, finding himself growing old, and much oppressed with sickness, would not have wished· to undertake any work that he no longer felt himself able to complete without almost compromising his former reputation. We may therefore suppose that the painting of Francis's mistress, " La belle Furoniere," is the work of some of his scholars.

Towards the latter end of his life, Leonardo's health was so much broken, that his infirmities no longer permitted him to take any part in the pleasures of the world, and he began to prepare himself for that awful change which he expected to be soon called upon to make. Vasari tells us, that believing himself near death, Da Vinci devoted the remainder of his days to

a more strict observance of the precepts of the Ca-
tholic religion ; which would almost imply that he had
lived the greater part of his life without any.   But this
inference is strongly contradicted by the morality and
propriety of his general conduct.   For although his
person, talents, and accomplishments would have given
him every probability of success, particularly when
united with the example of a most libertine court, it is
well known there was no man of his time less addicted
to gallantry and intrigue.   His writings also are all of
a more serious nature than could have been expected
from the vivacity of his disposition in early life.   And
even his paintings are entirely free from any sort of
lascivious or indecent ideas.   He seldom painted naked
figures ; but whenever he did undertake such subjects,
they were always remarkable for the purity and modesty of their attitudes ; as in the Leda, which is mentioned by Lomazzo, where he painted the eyes cast
down from shame.   Vasari must, therefore, have intended to express a total abandonment of the present
to fix his mind exclusively on the future, rather than
to insinuate any want of religion in his youth.   Naturally enthusiastic in his feelings, he turned his
thoughts to his Maker with the same ardour which
had distinguished him in all his actions ; and his death
was as glorious as his life had been virtuous and useful.
Having accompanied the court to Fontainbleau, he
expired in the arms of Francis the First, who came to
visit him during his illness, and happened by accident
to be with him when he was seized with a mortal
paroxysm that speedily terminated his existence.
What a triumph to the arts ! and what an honour to
the King ! who had the pleasing remembrance of

having comforted the last moments of one of the greatest artists that had then enlightened the world; and Francis must have looked back with more real satisfaction and self-approbation, to the recollection of his having supported and soothed Leonardo da Vinci in the hour of death, than to many of the more brilliant events of his reign. If at such a moment, when all artificial distinctions are at an end, Leonardo could have entertained one worldly thought, it must have alleviated his sufferings and encouraged his hopes, to know that he breathed out his soul in the arms of one of the greatest monarchs in Europe, who, while living, regarded him with the warmest admiration, and when dying lamented him with the sincerest regret.

Such was the enviable fate of Leonardo da Vinci, who died at the age of seventy-five, universally esteemed and as universally regretted. His whole life was spent in advancing the happiness of his fellow-creatures by furthering the progress of science. Few men have done more good in the world : a generous patron, an affectionate friend, and a liberal-minded man, he was as ready to promote the views of others as he was to acknowledge their merit ; and he had scarcely a wish beyond the advancement of general knowledge and the encouragement of the fine arts.

Several authors, and among others Ammoretti, attempt to deprive Leonardo of the honour of having died in the arms of Francis, which they treat as a fictitious story invented to amuse the lovers of the marvellous; but it is too well confirmed by contemporary writers and general tradition to be destroyed by these sceptics. We have, moreover, the testimony of Va-

sari, who relates the circumstance in these words :—
" At length, seeing himself near death, he confessed
himself with much contrition; and although he was
unable to stand, he desired his friends and servants to
support him, that he might receive the holy sacrament
out of bed in a more reverent posture. When fatigued
with this exertion, the King came to visit him, and
Leonardo, raising himself up in his bed out of respect
to his Majesty, began to relate the circumstances of
his illness, and the wrongs he had done both to God
and man, by not making better use of his talents. In
the midst of this conversation he was seized with a
paroxysm, which proved the messenger of death; on
seeing which, the King hastened to assist him, and
supported him in his bed, in order to alleviate his sufferings. But his divine spirit, knowing he could not
receive greater honour, expired in the King's arms
in the seventy-fifth year of his age."

Leonardo's having made his will at Amboise, is no
proof of his having died at Cloux, particularly as it
was written some months before his death. And as it
is well known that Fontainbleau was the favourite residence of Francis, there is every reason to suppose
that he would have desired Leonardo's assistance in the
embellishment of that place. As he was also attached
to the court and to the King personally, he would in
all probability have been wherever his master was.
Another reason Ammoretti gives for discrediting this
anecdote, is the circumstance of Francesco Melzi's
having written from Amboise to inform Da Vinci's
brothers of his death. But is it not possible, and even
probable, that Melzi, as his executor, should have gone
to the place where his effects were, and of which he
had also to give an account? At any rate, this story

is too pleasing a fiction, if it be one, to be slightly
discredited; and few would wish to disbelieve what
tradition has handed down to us, what all the poets
and painters who have since touched on the subject
have confirmed, and what is besides as glorious to
Leonardo, as it is creditable to Francis.

To a noble presence and beautiful countenance, Da
Vinci united uncommon strength both of body and
mind. His eloquence was so persuasive, that Vasari
says, " Con le parole sue volgeva al sì e al no ogn'
indurata intentione;" and his physical force was so
great, that he could bend a horse-shoe as if it were
lead. He was very magnificent in his attire, and
rather too fond of adorning his person in early life ;
but these foibles were more than counterbalanced by
the hospitality and liberality of his disposition. The
founder of an academy over which he presided for
some years, he may be supposed to have left a great
many literary works, which are most of them in manuscript, and preserved in different public libraries
throughout Europe. Among these are a treatise on
Hydraulics, with designs, another on Anatomy, and
another on the Anatomy of the Horse, which is noticed
by Vasari, Borghini, and Lomazzo ; and a treatise on
Perspective and on Light and Shade. But his best-
known work is the Trattato della Pittura, of which
there are several editions; an old one with etchings
by Stefano della Bella, and a more recent one printed
at Paris by Du Fresne in 1651, with figures by Nico-
las Poussin. This was translated into English and
published in London by John Senex in 1721. The en-
suing translation, by Rigaud, was first published in
London in 1802.

As an engineer, the canal of the Martesana, by

which he conducted the waters of the Adda to the
walls of Milan, a distance of nearly two hundred miles,
would have been alone sufficient to establish his reputation.   In this great work he obliged the impediments
of nature to give way to the efforts of genius, and he
succeeded to the admiration of all Italy.

As a painter, Leonardo da Vinci may be considered
the first who reconciled minute finishing with grandeur of design and harmony of expression.   His was
the very poetry of painting.   His exquisite taste, by
continually making him dissatisfied with his works,
urged him on to a nearer approach to perfection than
had ever been attained.   For this reason his scholars
were superior to those of any other master, as he
exacted from them the same profound attention to
nature, and laborious minuteness of style, which distinguished himself.

It is to be remembered, to the immortal honour of
Leonardo da Vinci, that he first dissipated the film of
ignorance which impeded the progress of the arts;
and if Raffaelle and Michael Angelo afterwards surpassed him in his own line, it is to him that justly
belongs the merit of having first pointed out the road
which they so successfully followed.   It is easier to
improve than to invent; but to him who had the
talents to imagine and the courage to overcome the
prejudices of ages, ought to belong the gratitude of
posterity, more than to those who, by following his
precepts, increased their own reputation.   To no one,
in short, are the arts more largely indebted than to
Leonardo da Vinci, whose virtues endeared him to all
who knew him, and whose exertions so mainly contributed to the refinement and civilization of future
ages.

CATALOGUE

WORKS PAINTED BY LEONARDO DA VINCI.

———————

IT is difficult to give a correct catalogue of the works of any artist who lived at so distant a period as Leonardo da Vinci, and also to point out the different places where they are to be found, with the names of their respective owners : the more so, as works of art, as well as states and kingdoms, have so frequently changed masters of late years, that it is almost impossible to trace them through so many revolutions.

The most considerable of Leonardo's undertakings were those painted on the walls of the refectory in the Convent of the Madonna della Grazia, at Milan ; but, unfortunately, little remains of them to establish his fame in the present day. His grand painting of "The Last Supper," and his portraits of the Duke Ludovico il Moro, the Duchess Beatrice, and their children, are nearly defaced ; and in addition to the ravages of time, the figure of our Saviour, which he painted on the wall, is destroyed by the enlargement of a doorway.

At the Canonica de Vaprio, he painted his own portrait by the side of a window, in the house of his friends the Melzi ; and in Vaprio, his colossal painting of the Virgin Mary is still to be seen in the palace belonging to the same family. In Rome he painted a figure of the Virgin on the wall of the cloisters in the Convent of St.

Onofrio. But of all these little remains but the outlines, from the circumstance of their having been painted on walls, and as difficult to remove as to preserve.

His oil paintings are much more numerous, as he painted on wood, on canvass, and on paper. As Milan was the place where he resided longest, it may be supposed that he painted most of his pictures there; but the greater part of those which could be removed, have long since been transported into other countries.

In the Public Gallery of *Milan*, are the portraits of the Duchess Beatrice and the Duke Maximilian. Another copy of the latter is in the Melzi Gallery. There is also the portrait of an Old Man, and a half figure of St. John the Baptist, which is considered as Leonardo's work, in the Public Gallery; but by some authors they are supposed to be only painted on his outlines.

In the Archbishop's Palace, a Virgin and Child, unfinished.

In the Palazzo Belgioso, a Holy Family that was at Piacenza; and innumerable smaller pictures dispersed among the private collections in Milan, most of which have now found their way to England.

At Isola Bella, in the possession of the Boromeo family, there is a half figure of a Young Man, in very good preservation.

At Bologna.

In the Hall of the Gonfaloniere, the portrait of a Boy.

At Florence.

In the Public Gallery.—The Medusa's Head. A small picture in the Tribune representing Herodias receiving the head of St. John the Baptist: by some this picture is attributed to Luino. The outlines, or rather the unfinished sketch of a large painting, representing the Epiphany, in the Scuola Fiorentina. And his own portrait, in the Hall of the Painters.

In the Palazzo Pitti, a Magdalen; most beautiful.

In the Palazzo Nicolini, the portrait of a Man.

In the Mozzi Gallery, the portrait of a Lady.

In the possession of Signor Fineschi is the famous picture of the Angel, described by Vasari, from the collection in the Palazzo Vecchio. This picture was for sale in 1828.

Rome.

In the Palazzo Borghese, a Holy Family. This is considered one of Leonardo's best pictures, and formerly belonged to Pope Clement the Seventh.

Palazzo Aldobrandini.—Jesus Christ disputing with the Doctors of Law : and the celebrated painting of La Vanità et la Modestia. The former picture is now in the National Gallery in London, and the latter was in 1828 in the possession of the late Earl of Dudley.

In the Giustiniani Gallery, a Holy Family; now in England, in the collection of the Earl of Suffolk.

A very fine portrait of a Lady was in the possession of the late Count D'Albany; and there was also a St. John in the collection of the Signora Angelica Kauffmann ; but these pictures are both removed ; the latter probably to Spain.

In Germany.

In the Imperial Gallery at Vienna—a picture of the Birth of our Saviour ; and an Herodias.

In the collection of Prince Kaunitz, the celebrated Leda.

In the Gallery of Prince Lichtenstein, the Head of our Saviour. This is the picture so much praised by Winkelman as a model of manly beauty.

At Dresden, in the Public Gallery, the portrait of Gian Jacopo Triulzio, General of the French army under Francis I.

At Munich, in the Public Gallery, a painting of the Virgin.

In the Royal Collection at Berlin, a very fine picture of Vertumnus and Pomona.

Russia.

At St. Petersburgh, in the Emperor's collection at the Hermitage, a Holy Family.

There are several smaller pictures of less note, which are considered as the work of his scholars, some of them perhaps finished upon his outlines.

Spain.

At Madrid, in the Royal Gallery—Jesus Christ brought before Pilate. Two pictures of the Virgin. A Head of St. John. This is most probably the picture that was in the collection of the Signora Angelica Kauffmann, as most of her pictures were sent to Spain. A San Girolamo in the grotto.

France.

At Paris, in the Louvre—the portrait of Mona Lisa, wife of Francesco del Giocondo, a Florentine, usually called "La belle Joconde." This is generally considered as Leonardo's best work. It was purchased by Francis I. for four thousand gold crowns, a sum which would now be equal to forty-five thousand francs. In the back-ground is a landscape. Sir Abraham Hume, Bart., has a copy of this picture.

The portrait of a Lady, supposed to be Lucretia Crevelli. She is dressed in red.

A St. John holding the cross in one hand, and pointing to heaven with the other.

A Holy Family, representing the infant Jesus giving his benediction to St. John, who is presented to him by Elizabeth. This picture is engraved by Desnayers.

A Holy Family, representing the Archangel Michael presenting Jesus the scales to weigh the good and evil actions of man : he is seated on the Virgin's lap, and they are both looking at Elizabeth and John the Baptist playing with a lamb.

Two pictures called Leonardo's, which are attributed rather to his school than to himself. One is St. John presenting the Cross of rushes to our Saviour. The other is St. Catharine of Alexandria at prayers.

A picture of the Virgin Mary sitting on the lap of Santa Anna, our Saviour and St. John playing at their feet. This is undoubtedly an original of Leonardo's : but has suffered very much from being over-cleaned, and is now greatly discoloured.

The Chevalier Gault relates that Monsieur de Chamois possesses one of Da Vinci's pictures representing Joseph and Potiphar's wife. He also says there is a group of Contadini in the Royal Gallery, but it exists there no longer.

The portrait of King Charles the Eighth of France, who died in 1497, for some time attributed to Leonardo, is now considered as the work of Perugino.

There are also several pictures in private collections in Paris, esteemed the works of Leonardo da Vinci ; but the author has endeavoured to name only those which are well known, and can be easily traced.

A picture has lately been discovered at Fontainebleau, which had long been given up as lost; the subject is Leda, and it is spoken of in the highest terms of praise.

In England.

The picture of Christ disputing with the Doctors of Law, formerly in the Aldobrandini Palace at Rome, is now in the National Gallery, having been bequeathed by the Rev. Holwell Carr, who purchased it from Lord Northwick, for 3,000 guineas.

La Colombina—purchased for 250 guineas by Robert Udney, Esq. from the Orleans collection.

The Virgin, Child, and Angels, from the Escurial palace, in the collection of Lord Ashburton.

Portrait of Mona Lisa, the wife of Francesco del Giocondo, in the collection of Sir Abraham Hume, Bart. This picture is a repetition of the one at Paris, and, although a very fine painting, is not equal to it.

At Stowe, in the collection of his Grace the Duke of Buckingham, a Holy Family.

A Holy Family, in excellent preservation, and one of Leonardo's best compositions. This picture was purchased from Mr. Justice Crawley, of Luton in Bedfordshire, and came originally from Italy. It was lately in the possession of Mess. Woodburn, of St. Martin's-lane, who have caused it to be engraved, and have sold the picture to an English Nobleman. A smaller picture on this subject, said to be painted by Da Vinci, is in the Fitzwilliam Collection at Cambridge.

In the collection of the late Duke of Bridgewater, was the portrait of a Woman, purchased by his Grace from the Orleans Collection, for 60 guineas, which is now in the possession of Lord Francis Egerton, at Cleveland House.

Herodias, in the Orleans collection, passed into the possession of Edward Coxe, esq. of Hampstead, and was sold again at his sale.

A Laughing Boy, with a play-thing in his hand. Nothing can exceed the masterly execution of this picture. It has the correctness of Raphael's drawing, and the graces and softness of Correggio's pencil. This picture was in the Arundel Collection, inherited by Lady Betty Germaine, who bequeathed it to Sir William Hamilton ; at whose sale, in April, 1801, it was purchased by Mr. Beckford for 1365l. It was at Fonthill, and is now at the Duke of Hamilton's. There are two drawings after the same Boy in the drawing book of Leonardo da Vinci, in the Ambrosian Library at Milan.

The Holy Family, that was in the Giustiniani Palace at Rome, is now in England in the collection of the Earl of Suffolk, at his seat at Charlton, near Malmesbury.

The picture of the Conception, originally in the church of San Francesco at Milan, is likewise in this country.

A fine picture of Francis I. in the character of our Saviour, was in 1828, in the possession of H. C. Andrews, Esq. of Sloane-street.

———

Several of the scholars of Leonardo da Vinci painted so like himself, that many of the pictures attributed to him belong more properly to his school, as his own occupations were so various that he could not possibly have painted all the pictures that are reputed to be his own works.

DRAWINGS.

A volume of valuable Drawings by Leonardo da Vinci, once the property of Pompeo Leoni, is now in the possession of his Britannic Majesty, and is at present kept at Cumberland Lodge. In it are contained 234 leaves, on which are pasted 779 drawings. It consists " of a variety of elegant heads, some of which are drawn with red and black chalks, on blue or red paper; others with a metal pencil on a tinted paper; a few of them are washed and heightened with white, and many are on common paper. The subjects are miscellaneous, as portraits, caricatures, single figures, tilting, horses, and other animals; botany, optics, perspective, gunnery, hydraulics, mechanics, and a great number of anatomical subjects, which are drawn with a more spirited pen, and illustrated with a variety of manuscript notes in his usual left-hand writing, in very fair characters. This volume contains the very characteristic portrait of Da Vinci, by himself, which was engraved by Bartolozzi;* together with sixteen other subjects, as male and female heads, characters, and caricatures; and published by Mr. Chamberlaine under royal patronage.

His Majesty's drawing of the Lord's Supper is accurately executed on paper with black lead, and highly finished; and formerly did honor to the Bonfiglioli collection at Bologna. †

* Chamberlaine's Life of Da Vinci, p. 11.
† Rogers' "Collection of Prints in imitation of Drawings, 1778," in which work is a copy in imitation of this drawing of the Last Supper, "W. W. Ryland sc. 1768."

In 1778, Robert Udney, esq. possessed a collection of 11 admirable Cartoons, containing 13 Heads in the Last Supper, which had been bought by the Procurator Sagredo at Venice, with the rest of the Marquis of Casinidi's collection.*   These were bought at Mr. Udney's sale by the late Mr. Woodburn, who sold them to the Duke of Hamilton ; the latter bequeathed them to the Duke of Somerset, in whose possession the greater part, if not the whole, are at present.

In the collection bequeathed to the British Museum by Richard Payne Knight, esq., are three small drawings by Leonardo da Vinci ; 1. a front portrait of Artus, chamberlain of Francis the First, remarkably fine ; 2. another, a profile head, fine ; and 3. in pen and ink, a fanciful battle of monsters, a dragon, a bear, an unicorn, &c. A seated figure holds a shield, on which is reflected the sun, which is seen raging in the sky.

A valuable series of Leonardo's Drawings for the " Last Supper," which was in the Ambrosian Library at Milan, has since been purchased by Sir Thomas Baring, Bart. They were afterwards bought of Sir T. Baring by the late Sir Thomas Lawrence. As that grand painting is so much destroyed, these drawings are of the highest interest. They have since, with about forty other drawings by Leonardo da Vinci, and the whole of Sir T. Lawrence's collection, come into the possession of Mess. Woodburn, St. Martin's-lane. One of Leonardo's drawings for the Last Supper, is still in the Ambrosian Library at Milan. The late Sir T. Lawrence was desirous of adding it to his collection.

* Rogers's " Prints in Imitation of Drawings," vol. i. p. 9.

f

MANUSCRIPTS.

Fourteen MS. volumes by Leonardo da Vinci are in the National Library at Paris, whither they were removed from the Ambrosian Library at Milan. J. B. Venturi (p. 4.) says, that they contain speculations in those branches of natural philosophy nearest allied to geometry; that they are first sketches and occasional notes, the author always intending afterwards to compose from them complete treatises. They are written backwards from right to left, in the manner of the oriental writers, probably with intention that the curious should not rob him of his discoveries. The spirit of geometry guided him throughout, whether it were in the art of analysing a subject in the connexion of the discourse, or the care of always generalizing his ideas. As to natural philosophy, he never was satisfied on any proposition if he had not proved it by experiment. Venturi has given extracts from Da Vinci's MSS. arranged under the following heads : Sect. 1. Of the descent of heavy bodies, combined with the rotation of the earth. 2. Of the earth divided into particles. 3. Of the earth and the moon. 4. Of the action of the sun on the sea. 5. Of the ancient state of the earth. 6. Of the flame and the air. 7. Of statics. 8. Of the descent of heavy bodies by inclined planes. 9. Of the water which one draws from a canal. 10. Of whirlpools. 11. Of vision. 12. Of military architecture. 13. Of some instruments. 14. Two chemical processes. 15. Of method.

In the Arundel collection of MSS. in the British Museum, No. 263 is a paper Volume in 8vo, ff. 283, written backwards, and illustrated by diagrams and delineations. It is his rough book of observations and demonstrations on subjects chiefly of mixed mathematics; being unconnected notes written by him at different times, commencing 22 March 1508, on the mechanical powers of forces, percussion, gravity, motion, optics, astronomy, &c. with various arithmetical and geometrical propositions in Italian. Several memoranda occur in this volume, (noticed in the printed Catalogue of the Arundel MSS. p. 79,) particularly the death of his father Pietro da Vinci.

LIST OF LEONARDO DA VINCI'S SCHOLARS, COLLECTED FROM HIS OWN NOTES AND MANUSCRIPTS.

Francesco Melzi.
Andrea Salaj'no, known in England by the name of Solario.
Marco Oggioni.
Gian Antonio Beltraffio.
Cesare da Sesto.
Pietro Ricci detto Gianpedrino.
Lorenzo Lotto.
Nicolo Appiano.

Bernardino Foxolo, Fanfoya, Jachomo, and Bernardino Luino, who was not his scholar, properly speaking, but who painted after his manner, studied him closely, and coloured a great many of his drawings and cartoons, with almost as much grace and softness as he could have done himself.

Lomazzo was more his friend and contemporary than his scholar, although he derived great benefit from his instructions.

MEMOIR

JOHN FRANCIS RIGAUD, ESQ. R.A.

JOHN FRANCIS RIGAUD, (whose excellent Translation of the Treatise on Painting, by Leonardo da Vinci, forms the principal part of this Volume,) was born at Turin, in the kingdom of Sardinia, on the 18th of May, 1742. His father was a respectable merchant, the descendant of a Protestant family, which had left France at the revocation of the Edict of Nantz, and had settled at Turin, where they flourished among the first merchants of that celebrated city.

It was intended that the subject of this narrative should have followed the mercantile vocation of his father; and, for that purpose, he had been brought into the counting-house; but, manifesting an unconquerable love for the art of painting, his father liberally consented to indulge his inclination, and afforded him every possible facility for prosecuting his favourite study. He immedi-

ately placed him under the care of one of the first
Artists of that day, the Chevalier Beaumont, principal Painter to the King of Sardinia.   Under his
instructions he made rapid progress ; and leaving
Turin, when properly grounded in the art, he
set out on his travels to visit the principal
cities of Italy, to examine the most celebrated
pictures of the great Masters; and, with that
view, he stopped principally at Rome, at Bologna, and at Parma, where he successfully copied
the famous picture of St. Jerome, by Corregio ;
and, in consequence of his merit, he was elected,
in 1766, a Member of the Clementine Academy of
Bologna. In 1772 he left Italy, and visited Paris,
where he had offers of considerable employment :
but his thirst for knowledge and fame being predo-
minant, he rejected the patronage that was offered
to him, determined to see the productions of the
British School, and partake of the advantages of
the establishment of the Royal Academy at London; of which he hoped to become, by his assiduity and abilities, a deserving Member.   The
first Picture that he exhibited in England, was
the HERCULES, which secured him great praise.
In November of the same year, he was elected an
Associate : and in 1785 he was chosen a Royal
Academician.

From the moment he received his first academic
honours in this country he was determined to settle
in it, and continued to follow the Historic line of

Painting, which was his great delight; occasionally
painting Portraits, which he undertook with reluct-
ance, regretting every moment that was not employed in the higher department of Art.

Always anxious for improvement, he left England in the year 1782, to make a tour through
Flanders and Germany, visiting all the great Collections: and having thus gratified himself with
the sight of them, he explored the grand beauties
of Nature in Switzerland. From Switzerland he
returned to England, and from that time continued the exercise of his professional talents
with vigour and diligence. He painted some ceil-
ings, which then, fortunately for Art, was the
fashion of the time; particularly one for the late
Marquis of Donegal, at Fisherwick; the Library
at Packington, in encaustic, for the present Earl
of Aylesford; and the ceiling of the Court Room
at the Trinity House, on Tower Hill.

Having studied so much in Italy, where Fresco
Painting was still practised, he was completely acquainted with its process; and, by the encouragement of the Earl of Aylesford, who honoured him
with his friendship and patronage, he was induced
to paint for his Lordship an Altar-piece, in Fresco,
for the Parish Church at Packington, his Lordship's Seat in Warwickshire; which is supposed
to be the first Painting in Fresco executed in this
country. He painted another Altar-piece, after
the same manner, for the Parish Church of St.

Martin Outwich, in the city of London. His celebrated Picture of the Exposing of Moses, was so much admired by a Swedish gentleman, then on his travels in England, that he ordered a duplicate, which was taken to Stockholm; and such was the impression it made in that city, that he was not only immediately elected a Member of its Royal Academy, but was appointed Historical Painter to the King of Sweden. In England he was employed in those great undertakings, the Poets, Shakspeare, and Historic Galleries.

His love for Painting was not evinced by his pencil only, his pen was also engaged in its service; for he made an excellent translation of the Treatise on Painting by Leonardo da Vinci, and wrote an Essay for the periodical publication intitled "The Artist," on the materials for Painting.

He continued in the perfect enjoyment of his faculties, and in the full exercise of his Art, until the very last moment of his life; and he died as tranquilly as he had lived honourably; he was found dead in his bed, at the Seat of the Earl of Aylesford, at Packington in Warwickshire, on the 6th of December 1810, in the sixty-ninth year of his age.

As an Artist, his Works will convey his name with high respect to posterity. Many of his best Easel Pictures were comprised in a Sale of his Collection by Mr. Peter Coxe, April 3, 1811, (wh prefixed to the Catalogue this memoir, of which we gladly avail ourselves.)

As a man, he was an agreable member of society, had a rich fund of general knowledge, and showed an urbanity of manners which rendered him universally pleasing: the recollection of which will endear his memory to all who had the happiness of knowing him. He was eminently upright, of quick sensibility, warm and sincere in friendship, a good husband, and an excellent father.

A portrait of Mr. Rigaud, drawn by George Dance, R.A. in 1793, and engraved by William Daniel, R.A., will be found in the second volume of Dance's Collection of Portraits, fol. 1814.

Throgmorton Street, 1811.

A

TREATISE ON PAINTING.

DRAWING.

PROPORTION.

CHAP. I.—*What the young Student in Painting
ought in the first place to learn.*

THE young student should, in the first place,
acquire a knowledge of perspective, to enable him
to give to every object its proper dimensions : after
which, it is requisite that he be under the care of
an able master, to accustom him, by degrees, to a
good style of drawing the parts.   Next, he must
study Nature, in order to confirm and fix in his
mind the reason of those precepts which he has
learnt.   He must also bestow some time in viewing
the works of various old masters, to form his eye
and judgment, in order that he may be able to put
in practice all that he has been taught.*

---

* This passage has been by some persons much misunderstood,
and supposed to require, that the student should be a deep pro-

CHAP. II.—*Rule for a young Student in Painting.*

The organ of sight is one of the quickest, and takes in at a single glance an infinite variety of forms; notwithstanding which, it cannot perfectly comprehend more than one object at a time. For example, the reader, at one look over this page, immediately perceives it full of different characters; but he cannot at the same moment distinguish each letter, much less can he comprehend their meaning. He must consider it word by word, and line by line, if he be desirous of forming a just notion of these characters. In like manner, if we wish to ascend to the top of an edifice, we must be content to advance step by step, otherwise we shall never be able to attain it.

A young man, who has a natural inclination to the study of this art, I would advise to act thus: In order to acquire a true notion of the form of things, he must begin by studying the parts which compose them, and not pass to a second till he has well stored his memory, and sufficiently practised the first; otherwise he loses his time, and will most certainly protract his studies. And let him remember to acquire accuracy before he attempts quickness.

ficient in perspective, before he commences the study of painting; but it is a knowledge of the leading principles only of perspective that the author here means, and without such a knowledge, which is easily to be acquired, the student will inevitably fall into errors, as gross as those humourously pointed out by Hogarth, in his Frontispiece to Kirby's Perspective.

CHAP. III.—*How to discover a young Man's Disposition for Painting.*

Many are very desirous of learning to draw, and are very fond of it, who are, notwithstanding, void of a proper disposition for it. This may be known by their want of perseverance; like boys, who draw every thing in a hurry, never finishing, or shadowing.

CHAP. IV.—*Of Painting, and its Divisions.*

Painting is divided into two principal parts. The first is the figure, that is, the lines which distinguish the forms of bodies, and their component parts. The second is the colour contained within those limits.

CHAP. V.—*Division of the Figure.*

The form of bodies is divided into two parts; that is, the proportion of the members to each other, which must correspond with the whole; and the motion, expressive of what passes in the mind of the living figure.

CHAP. VI.—*Proportion of Members.*

The proportion of members is again divided into two parts, viz. equality, and motion. By equality is meant (besides the measure corresponding with the whole), that you do not confound the members of a young subject with those of old age, nor plump ones with those that are lean; and that, moreover, you do not blend the robust and firm muscles of man with feminine softness: that the attitudes and motions of old age be not expressed with the quickness and alacrity of youth; nor those of a female figure like those of a vigorous young man. The motions and members of a strong man should be such as to express his perfect state of health.

CHAP. VII.—*Of Dimensions in general.*

In general, the dimensions of the human body are to be considered in the length, and not in the breadth; because in the wonderful works of Nature, which we endeavour to imitate, we cannot in any species find any one part in one model precisely similar to the same part in another. Let us be attentive, therefore, to the variation of forms, and avoid all monstrosities of proportion; such as long legs united to short bodies, and narrow chests with long arms. Observe also attentively the measure of joints, in which Nature is apt to vary considerably; and imitate her example by doing the same.

CHAP. VIII.—*Motion, Changes, and Proportion of Members.*

The measures of the human body vary in each member, according as it is more or less bent, or seen in different views, increasing on one side as much as they diminish on the other.

Chap. IX.—*The Difference of Proportion be-. tween Children and grown Men.*

In men and children I find a great difference between the joints of the one and the other, in the length of the bones. A man has the length of two heads from the extremity of one shoulder to the other, the same from the shoulder to the elbow, and from the elbow to the fingers; but the child has only one, because Nature gives the proper size first to the seat of the intellect, and afterwards to the other parts.

Chap. X.—*The Alterations in the Proportion of the human Body from Infancy to full Age.*

A man, in his infancy, has the breadth of his shoulders equal to the length of the face, and to the length of the arm from the shoulder to the elbow, when the arm is bent.* It is the same again from the lower belly to the knee, and from the knee to the foot. But, when a man is arrived at the period of his full growth, every one of these dimensions becomes double in length, except the face, which, with the top of the head, undergoes but very little alteration in length. A well-proportioned and full-grown man, therefore, is ten times the length of his face; the breadth of his shoulders will be two faces, and in like manner all the above lengths will be double. The rest will

* See Chap. cccll.

be explained in the general measurement of the
human body.*

CHAP. XI.—*Of the Proportion of Members.*

All the parts of any animal whatever must be
correspondent with the whole. So that, if the body
be short and thick, all the members belonging to
it must be the same. One that is long and thin
must have its parts of the same kind; and so of
the middle size. Something of the same may be
observed in plants, when uninjured by men or
tempests: for, when thus injured they bud and
grow again, making young shoots from old plants,
and by those means destroying their natural symmetry.

CHAP. XII.—*That every Part be proportioned
to its Whole.*

If a man be short and thick, be careful that all
his members be of the same nature, viz. short
arms and thick, large hands, short fingers, with
broad joints; and so of the rest.

CHAP. XIII.—*Of the Proportion of the Members.*

Measure upon yourself the proportion of the
parts, and, if you find any of them defective, note
it down, and be very careful to avoid it in drawing
your own compositions. For this is reckoned a
common fault in painters, to delight in the imitation of themselves.

* Not to be found in this work.

CHAP. XIV.—*The Danger of forming an erro-neous Judgment in regard to the Proportion and Beauty of the Parts.*

If the painter has clumsy hands, he will be apt to introduce them into his works, and so of any other part of his person, which may not happen to be so beautiful as it ought to be. He must, there-fore, guard particularly against that self-love, or too good opinion of his own person, and study by every means to acquire the knowledge of what is most beautiful, and of his own defects, that he may adopt the one and avoid the other.

CHAP. XV.—*Another Precept.*

The young painter must, in the first instance, accustom his hand to copying the drawings of good masters; and when his hand is thus formed, and ready, he should, with the advice of his di-rector, use himself also to draw from relievos; according to the rules we shall point out in the treatise on drawing from relievos.*

* From this, and many other similar passages, it is evident, that the author intended at some future time to arrange his ma-nuscript collections, and to publish them as separate treatises. That he did not do so is well known; but it is also a fact, that, in selecting from the whole mass of his collections the chapters of which the present work consists, great care appears in general to have been taken to extract also those to which there was any re-ference from any of the chapters intended for this work, or which from their subject were necessarily connected with them. Accord-ingly, the reader will find, in the notes to this translation, that

CHAP. XVI.—*The Manner of drawing from Relievos, and rendering Paper fit for it.*

When you draw from relievos, tinge your paper of some darkish demi-tint. And after you have made your outline, put in the darkest shadows, and, last of all, the principal lights, but sparingly, especially the smaller ones; because those are easily lost to the eye at a very moderate distance.*

CHAP. XVII.—*Of drawing from Casts or Nature.*

In drawing from relievo, the draftsman must place himself in such a manner, as that the eye of the figure to be drawn be level with his own.†

all such chapters in any other part of the present work are uniformly pointed out, as have any relation to the respective passages in the text. This, which has never before been done, though indispensably necessary, will be found of singular use, and it was thought proper here, once for all, to notice it.

In the present instance the chapters, referring to the subject in the text, are Chap. XV. XVII. XVIII. XIX. XX. XXVI.; and though these do not afford complete information, yet it is to be remembered, that drawing from relievos is subject to the very same rules as drawing from Nature; and that, therefore, what is elsewhere said on that subject is also equally applicable to this.

* The meaning of this is, that the last touches of light, such as the shining parts (which are always narrow), must be given sparingly. In short, that the drawing must be kept in broad masses as much as possible.

† This is not an absolute rule, but it is a very good one for drawing of portraits.

Chap. XVIII.—*To draw Figures from Nature.*

Accustom yourself to hold a plummet in your hand, that you may judge of the bearing of the parts.

Chap. XIX.—*Of drawing from Nature.*

When you draw from Nature, you must be at the distance of three times the height of the object; and when you begin to draw, form in your own mind a certain principal line (suppose a perpendicular); observe well the bearing of the parts towards that line; whether they intersect it, are parallel to it or oblique.

Chap. XX.—*Of drawing Academy Figures.*

When you draw from a naked model, always sketch in the whole of the figure, suiting all the members well to each other; and though you finish only that part which appears the best, have a regard to the rest, that, whenever you make use of such studies, all the parts may hang together.

In composing your attitudes, take care not to turn the head on the same side as the breast, nor let the arm go in a line with the leg.* If the head turn towards the right shoulder, the parts must be lower on the left side than on the other: but if the chest come forward, and the head turn towards the left, the parts on the right side are to be the highest.

* See Chap. ci.

B 5

CHAP. XXI.—*Of studying in the Dark, on first waking in the Morning, and before going to sleep.*

I have experienced no small benefit, when in the dark and in bed, by retracing in my mind the outlines of those forms which I had previously studied, particularly such as had appeared the most difficult to comprehend and retain; by this method they will be confirmed and treasured up in the memory.

CHAP. XXII.—*Observations on drawing Portraits.*

The cartilage, which raises the nose in the middle of the face, varies in eight different ways. It is equally straight, equally concave, or equally convex, which is the first sort. Or, secondly, unequally straight, concave, or convex. Or, thirdly, straight in the upper part, and concave in the under. Or, fourthly, straight again in the upper part, and convex in those below. Or, fifthly, it may be concave and straight beneath. Or, sixthly, concave above, and convex below. Or, seventhly, it may be convex in the upper part, and straight in the lower. And in the eighth and last place, convex above, and concave beneath.

The uniting of the nose with the brows is in two ways, either it is straight or concave. The forehead has three different forms. It is straight, concave, or round. The first is divided into two parts, viz. it is either convex in the upper part, or in the lower, sometimes both; or else flat above and below.

CHAP. XXIII.—*The Method of retaining in the Memory the Likeness of a Man, so as to draw his Profile, after having seen him only once.*

You must observe and remember well the variations of the four principal features in the profile; the nose, mouth, chin, and forehead. And first of the nose, of which there are three different sorts,* straight, concave, and convex. Of the straight there are but four variations, short or long, high at the end, or low. Of the concave there are three sorts; some have the concavity above, some in the middle, and some at the end. The convex noses also vary three ways; some project in the upper part, some in the middle, and others at the bottom. Nature, which seems to delight in infinite variety, gives again three changes to those noses which have a projection in the middle; for some have it straight, some concave, and some convex.

CHAP. XXIV.—*How to remember the Form of a Face.*

If you wish to retain with facility the general look of a face, you must first learn how to draw well several faces, mouths, eyes, noses, chins, throats, necks, and shoulders; in short, all those principal parts which distinguish one man from another. For instance, noses are of ten different sorts :† straight, bunched, concave, some raised above, some below

---

* See the preceding chapter.
† See the two preceding chapters.

the middle, aqueline, flat, round, and sharp. These
affect the profile. In the front view there are eleven
different sorts. Even, thick in the middle, thin in
the middle, thick at the tip, thin at the beginning,
thin at the tip, and thick at the beginning. Broad,
narrow, high, and low nostrils; some with a large
opening, and some more shut towards the tip.

The same variety will be found in the other parts
of the face, which must be drawn from Nature,
and retained in the memory. Or else, when you
mean to draw a likeness from memory, take with
you a pocket-book, in which you have marked all
these variations of features, and after having given
a look at the face you mean to draw, retire a little
aside, and note down in your book which of the
features are similar to it; that you may put it all
together at home.

CHAP. XXV.—*That a Painter should take Plea-*
sure in the Opinion of every body.

A painter ought not certainly to refuse listening
to the opinion of any one; for we know that,
although a man be not a painter, he may have just
notions of the forms of men; whether a man has
a hump on his back, a thick leg, or a large hand;
whether he be lame, or have any other defect.
Now, if we know that men are able to judge of the
works of Nature, should we not think them more
able to detect our errors?

ANATOMY.

CHAP. XXVI.—*What is principally to be observed in Figures.*

The principal and most important consideration required in drawing figures, is to set the head well upon the shoulders, the chest upon the hips, the hips and shoulders upon the feet.

CHAP. XXVII.—*Mode of Studying.*

Study the science first, and then follow the practice which results from that science. Pursue method in your study, and do not quit one part till it be perfectly engraven in the memory; and observe what difference there is between the members of animals and their joints.*

CHAP. XXVIII.—*Of being universal.*

It is an easy matter for a man who is well versed in the principles of his art, to become universal in the practice of it, since all animals have a similarity of members, that is, muscles, tendons, bones, &c. These only vary in length or thickness, as will be demonstrated in the Anatomy.† As for aquatic animals, of which there is great variety, I shall not

* Man being the highest of the animal creation, ought to be the chief object of study.

† An intended Treatise, as it seems, on Anatomy, which however never was published; but there are several chapters in the present work on the subject of Anatomy, most of which will be

persuade the painter to take them as a rule, having no connexion with our purpose.

CHAP. XXIX.—*A Precept for the Painter.*

It reflects no great honour on a painter to be able to execute only one thing well, such as a head, an academy figure, or draperies, animals, landscape or the like, confining himself to some particular object of study; because there is scarcely a person so void of genius as to fail of success, if he apply earnestly to one branch of study, and practise it continually.

CHAP. XXX.—*Of the Measures of the human Body, and the bending of Members.*

It is very necessary that painters should have a knowledge of the bones which support the flesh by which they are covered, but particularly of the joints, which increase and diminish the length of them in their appearance. As in the arm, which does not measure the same when bent, as when extended; its difference between the greatest extension and bending, is about one eighth of its length. The increase and diminution of the arm is effected by the bone projecting out of its socket at the elbow; which, as is seen in figure A B,

found under the present head of Anatomy; and of such as could not be placed there, because they also related to some other branch, the following is a list by which they may be found: Chapters VI. VII. X. XI. XXXIV. XXXV. XXXVI. XXXVII. XXXVIII. XXXIX. XL. XLI. XLII. XLIII. XLIV. XLV. XLVI. XLVIII. XLIX. L. LI. LII. CXXIX.

Plate I. is lengthened from the shoulder to the elbow; the angle it forms being less than a right angle. It will appear longer as that angle becomes more acute, and will shorten in proportion as it becomes more open or obtuse.

CHAP. XXXI.—*Of the small Bones in several Joints of the human Body.*

There are in the joints of the human body certain small bones, fixed in the middle of the tendons which connect several of the joints. Such are the patellas of the knees and the joints of the shoulders, and those of the feet. They are eight in number, one at each shoulder, one at each knee, and two at each foot under the first joint of the great toe towards the heel. These grow extremely hard as a man advances in years.

CHAP. XXXII.—*Memorandum to be observed by the Painter.*

Note down which muscles and tendons are brought into action by the motion of any member, and when they are hidden. Remember that these remarks are of the greatest importance to painters and sculptors, who profess to study anatomy, and the science of the muscles. Do the same with children, following the different gradations of age from their birth even to decrepitude, describing the changes which the members, and particularly the joints, undergo; which of them grow fat, and which lean.

CHAP. XXXIII.—*The Shoulders.*

The joints of the shoulders, and other parts which bend, shall be noticed in their places in the Treatise on Anatomy, where the cause of the motions of all the parts which compose the human body shall be explained.*

CHAP. XXXIV.—*The Difference of Joints between Children and grown Men.*

Young children have all their joints small, but they are thick and plump in the spaces between them; because there is nothing upon the bones at the joints, but some tendons to bind the bones together. The soft flesh, which is full of fluids, is enclosed under the skin in the space between the joints; and as the bones are bigger at the joints than in the space between them, the skin throws off in the progress to manhood that superfluity, and draws nearer to the bones, thinning the whole part together. But upon the joints it does not lessen, as there is nothing but cartilages and tendons. For these reasons children are small in the joints, and plump in the space between, as may be observed in their fingers, arms, and narrow shoulders. Men, on the contrary, are large and full in the joints, in the arms and legs; and where children have hollows, men are knotty and prominent.

* See chap. LXXXVII.

CHAP. XXXV.—*Of the Joints of the Fingers.*

The joints of the fingers appear larger on all sides when they bend; the more they bend the larger they appear. The contrary is the case when straight. It is the same in the toes, and it will be more perceptible in proportion to their fleshiness.

CHAP. XXXVI.—*Of the Joint of the Wrist.*

The wrist or joint between the hand and arm lessens on closing the hand, and grows larger when it opens. The contrary happens in the arm, in the space between the elbow and the hand, on all sides; because in opening the hand the muscles are extended and thinned in the arm, from the elbow to the wrist; but when the hand is shut, the same muscles swell and shorten. The tendons alone start, being stretched by the clenching of the hand.

CHAP. XXXVII.—*Of the Joint of the Foot.*

The increase and diminution in the joint of the foot is produced on that side where the tendons are seen, as D E F, *Plate I.* which increases when the angle is acute, and diminishes when it becomes obtuse. It must be understood of the joint in the front part of the foot A B C.

CHAP. XXXVIII.—*Of the Knee.*

Of all the members which have pliable joints,

the knee is the only one that lessens in the bending, and becomes larger by extension.

Chap. XXXIX.—*Of the Joints.*

All the joints of the human body become larger by bending, except that of the leg.

Chap. XL.—*Of the Naked.*

When a figure is to appear nimble and delicate, its muscles must never be too much marked, nor are any of them to be much swelled. Because such figures are expressive of activity and swiftness, and are never loaded with much flesh upon the bones. They are made light by the want of flesh, and where there is but little flesh there cannot be any thickness of muscles.

Chap. XLI.—*Of the Thickness of the Muscles.*

Muscular men have large bones, and are in general thick and short, with very little fat; because the fleshy muscles in their growth contract closer together, and the fat, which in other instances lodges between them, has no room. The muscles in such thin subjects, not being able to extend, grow in thickness, particularly towards their middle, in the parts most removed from the extremities.

Chap. XLII.—*Fat Subjects have small Muscles.*

Though fat people have this in common with

muscular men, that they are frequently short and
thick, they have thin muscles; but their skin contains a great deal of spongy and soft flesh full of
air; for that reason they are lighter upon the
water, and swim better than muscular people.

CHAP. XLIII.—*Which of the Muscles disappear
in the Motions of the Body.*

In raising or lowering the arm, the pectoral
muscles disappear, or acquire a greater relievo. A
similar effect is produced by the hips, when they
bend either inwards or outwards. It is to be observed, that there is more variety of appearances
in the shoulders, hips, and neck, than in any other
joint, because they are susceptible of the greatest
variety of motions. But of this subject I shall
make a separate treatise*.

CHAP. XLIV.—*Of the Muscles.*

The muscles are not to be scrupulously marked
all the way, because it would be disagreeable to
the sight, and of very difficult execution. But on
that side only where the members are in action,
they should be pronounced more strongly; for
muscles that are at work naturally collect all their
parts together, to gain increase of strength, so that

* It does not appear that this intention was ever carried into
execution; but there are many chapters in this work on the subject of motion, where all that is necessary for a painter in this
branch will be found.

some small parts of those muscles will appear, that
were not seen before.

CHAP. XLV.—*Of the Muscles.*

The muscles of young men are not to be marked
strongly, nor too much swelled, because that would
indicate full strength and vigour of age, which they
have not yet attained. Nevertheless they must
be more or less expressed, as they are more or less
employed. For those which are in motion are
always more swelled and thicker than those which
remain at rest. The intrinsic and central line of
the members which are bent, never retains its
natural length.

CHAP. XLVI.—*The Extension and Contraction of the Muscles.*

The muscle at the back part of the thigh shows
more variety in its extension and contraction, than
any other in the human body; the second, in that
respect, are those which compose the buttocks;
the third, those of the back; the fourth, those of
the neck; the fifth, those of the shoulders; and the
sixth, those of the Abdomen, which, taking their
rise under the breast, terminate under the lower
belly; as I shall explain when I speak of each.

CHAP. XLVII.—*Of the Muscle between the Chest and the lower Belly.*

There is a muscle which begins under the breast

at the Sternum, and is inserted into, or terminates at the Os pubis, under the lower belly. It is called the Rectus of the Abdomen; it is divided, length-ways, into three principal portions, by transverse tendinous intersections or ligaments, viz. the supe-rior part, and a ligament; the second part, with its ligaments; and the third part, with the third ligament; which last unites by tendons to the Os pubis. These divisions and intersections of the same muscle are intended by nature to facilitate the motion when the body is bent or distended. If it were made of one piece, it would produce too much variety when extended, or contracted, and also would be considerably weaker. When this muscle has but little variety in the motion of the body, it is more beautiful.*

CHAP. XLVIII.—*Of a Man's complex Strength, but first of the Arm.*

The muscles which serve either to straighten or bend the arm, arise from the different processes of the Scapula; some of them from the protuberances of the Humerus, and others about the middle of

* Anatomists have divided this muscle into four or five sec-tions; but painters, following the ancient sculptors, show only the three principal ones; and, in fact, we find that a greater number of them (as may often be observed in nature) gives a dis-agreeable meagreness to the subject. Beautiful nature does not show more than three, though there may be more hid under the skin.

the Os humeri. The extensors of the arm arise from behind, and the flexors from before.

That a man has more power in pulling than in pushing, has been proved by the ninth proposition De Ponderibus,* where it is said, that of two equal weights, that will have the greatest power which is farthest removed from the pole or centre of its balance. It follows then of course, that the muscle N B, *Plate II.* and the muscle N C, being of equal power, the inner muscle N C, will nevertheless be stronger than the outward one N B, because it is inserted into the arm at C, a point farther removed from the centre of the elbow A, than B, which is on the other side of such centre, so that that question is determined. But this is a simple power, and I thought it best to explain it before I mentioned the complex power of the muscles, of which I must now take notice. The complex power, or strength, is, for instance, this, when the arm is going to act, a second power is added to it (such as the weight of the body and the strength of the legs, in pulling or pushing), consisting in the extension of the parts, as when two men attempt to throw down a column; the one by pushing, and the other by pulling.†

---

* A treatise on weights, like many others, intended by this author, but never published.

† See the next chapter.

CHAP. XLIX.—*In which of the two Actions, Pulling or Pushing, a Man has the greatest Power,* Plate II.

A man has the greatest power in pulling, for in that action he has the united exertion of all the muscles of the arm, while some of them must be inactive when he is pushing; because when the arm is extended for that purpose, the muscles which move the elbow cannot act, any more than if he pushed with his shoulders against the column he means to throw down; in which case only the muscles that extend the back, the legs under the thigh, and the calves of the legs, would be active. From which we conclude, that in pulling there is added to the power of extension the strength of the arms, of the legs, of the back, and even of the chest, if the oblique motion of the body require it. But in pushing, though all the parts were employed, yet the strength of the muscles of the arms is wanting; for to push with an extended arm without motion does not help more than if a piece of wood were placed from the shoulder to the column meant to be pushed down.

CHAP. L.—*Of the bending of Members, and of the Flesh round the bending Joint.*

The flesh which covers the bones near and at the joints, swells or diminishes in thickness according to their bending or extension; that is, it increases at the inside of the angle formed by the bending, and grows narrow and lengthened on the outward side of the exterior angle. The middle between the convex and concave angle participates of this increase or diminution, but in a greater or less degree as the parts are nearer to, or farther from, the angles of the bending joints.

CHAP. LI.—*Of the naked Body.*

The members of naked men who work hard in different attitudes, will show the muscles more strongly on that side where they act forcibly to bring the part into action; and the other muscles will be more or less marked, in proportion as they co-operate in the same motion.

CHAP. LII.—*Of a Ligament without Muscles.*

Where the arm joins with the hand, there is a ligament, the largest in the human body, which is without muscles, and is called the strong ligament of the Carpus; it has a square shape, and serves to bind and keep close together the bones of the arm, and the tendons of the fingers, and prevent their dilating, or starting out.

CHAP. LIII.—*Of Creases.*

In bending the joints the flesh will always form a crease on the opposite side to that where it is tight.

CHAP. LIV.—*How near behind the Back one Arm can be brought to the other*, Plate III. and IV.

When the arms are carried behind the back, the elbows can never be brought nearer than the length from the elbow to the end of the longest finger; so that the fingers will not be seen beyond the elbows, and in that situation, the arms with the shoulders form a perfect square. The greatest extension of the arm across the chest is, when the elbow comes over the pit of the stomach; the elbow and the shoulder in this position, will form an equilateral triangle.

CHAP. LV.—*Of the Muscles.*

A naked figure being strongly marked, so as to give a distinct view of all the muscles, will not express any motion; because it cannot move, if some of its muscles do not relax while the others are pulling. Those which relax cease to appear in proportion as the others pull strongly and become apparent.

CHAP. LVI.—*Of the Muscles.*

The muscles of the human body are to be more or less marked according to their degree of action. Those only which act are to be shewn, and the more forcibly they act, the stronger they should be pronounced. Those that do not act at all must remain soft and flat.

C

Chap. LVII.—*Of the Bending of the Body.*

The bodies of men diminish as much on the side which bends, as they increase on the opposite side. That diminution may at last become double, in proportion to the extension on the other side. But of this I shall make a separate treatise*.

Chap. LVIII.—*The same subject.*

The body which bends, lengthens as much on one side as it shortens on the other; but the central line between them will never lessen or increase.

Chap. LIX.—*The Necessity of anatomical Knowledge.*

The painter who has obtained a perfect knowledge of the nature of the tendons and muscles, and of those parts which contain the most of them, will know to a certainty, in giving a particular motion to any part of the body, which, and how many of the muscles give rise and contribute to it; which of them, by swelling, occasion their shortening, and which of the cartilages they surround.

He will not imitate those who, in all the different attitudes they adopt, or invent, make use of the same muscles, in the arms, back, or chest, or any other parts.

* It is believed that this treatise, like many others promised by the author, was never written.

MOTION AND EQUIPOISE OF FIGURES.

CHAP. LX.—*Of the Equipoise of a Figure standing still.*

The non-existence of motion in any animal resting on its feet, is owing to the equality of weight distributed on each side of the line of gravity.

CHAP. LXI.—*Motion produced by the Loss of Equilibrium.*

Motion is created by the loss of due equipoise, that is, by inequality of weight; for nothing can move of itself, without losing its centre of gravity, and the farther that is removed, the quicker and stronger will be the motion.

CHAP. LXII.—*Of the Equipoise of Bodies,* Plate V.

The balance or equipoise of parts in the human body is of two sorts, viz. simple and complex. Simple, when a man stands upon his feet without motion: in that situation, if he extends his arms at different distances from the middle, or stoop, the centre of his weight will always be in a perpendicular line upon the centre of that foot which supports the body; and if he rests equally upon both feet, then the middle of the chest will be per-

pendicular to the middle of the line which measures the space between the centres of his feet.

The complex balance is, when a man carries a
weight not his own, which he bears by different
motions; as in the figure of Hercules stifling Anteus, by pressing him against his breast with his
arms, after he has lifted him from the ground.
He must have as much of his own weight thrown
behind the central line of his feet, as the weight
of Anteus adds before.

Chap. LXIII.—*Of Positions.*

The pit of the neck, between the two clavicles,
falls perpendicularly with the foot which bears the
weight of the body.   If one of the arms be thrown
forwards, this pit will quit that perpendicular; and
if one of the legs goes back, that pit is brought
forwards, and so changes its situation at every
change of posture.

Chap. LXIV.—*Of balancing the Weight round the Centre of Gravity in Bodies.*

A figure standing upon its feet without motion,
will form an equipoise of all its members round
the centre of its support.

If this figure without motion, and resting upon
its feet, happens to move one of its arms forwards,
it must necessarily throw as much of its weight on
the opposite side, as is equal to that of the ex-

tended arm and the accidental weight. And the same I say of every part, which is brought out beyond its usual balance.

CHAP. LXV.—*Of Figures that have to lift up, or carry any Weight.*

A weight can never be lifted up or carried by any man, if he do not throw more than an equal weight of his own on the opposite side.

CHAP. LXVI.—*The Equilibrium of a Man standing upon his Feet,* Plate VI.

The weight of a man resting upon one leg will always be equally divided on each side of the central or perpendicular line of gravity, which supports him. .

CHAP. LXVII.—*Of Walking,* Plate VII.

A man walking will always have the centre of gravity over the centre of the leg which rests upon the ground.

CHAP. LXVIII.—*Of the Centre of Gravity in Men and Animals.*

The legs, or centre of support, in men and animals, will approach nearer to the centre of gravity, in proportion to the slowness of their motion; and, on the contrary, when the motion is quicker, they will be farther removed from that perpendicular line.

CHAP. LXIX.—*Of the corresponding Thickness of Parts on each Side of the Body.*

The thickness or breadth of the parts in the human body will never be equal on each side, if the corresponding members do not move equally and alike.

CHAP. LXX.—*Of the Motions of Animals.*

All bipeds in their motions lower the part immediately over the foot that is raised, more than over that resting on the ground, and the highest parts do just the contrary. This is observable in the hips and shoulders of a man when he walks; and also in birds in the head and rump.

CHAP. LXXI.—*Of Quadrupeds and their Motions.*

The highest parts of quadrupeds are susceptible of more variation when they walk, than when they are still, in a greater or less degree, in proportion to their size. This proceeds from the oblique position of their legs when they touch the ground, which raise the animal when they become straight and perpendicular upon the ground.

CHAP. LXXII.—*Of the Quickness or Slowness of Motion.*

The motion performed by a man, or any other animal whatever, in walking, will have more or less velocity as the centre of their weight is more or

less removed from the centre of that foot upon
which they are supported.

CHAP. LXXIII.—*Of the Motion of Animals.*

That figure will appear the swiftest in its course
which leans the most forwards.

Any body, moving of itself, will do it with more
or less velocity in proportion as the centre of its
gravity is more or less removed from the centre of
its support. This is mentioned chiefly in regard
to the motion of birds, which, without any clap-
ping of their wings, or assistance of wind, move
themselves. This happens when the centre of
their gravity is out of the centre of their support,
viz. out of its usual residence, the middle between
the two wings. Because, if the middle of the
wings be more backward than the centre of the
whole weight, the bird will move forwards and
downwards, in a greater or less degree as the
centre of its weight is more or less removed from
the middle of its wings. From which it follows,
that if the centre of gravity be far removed from
the other centre, the descent of the bird will be
very oblique; but if that centre be near the middle
of the wings, the descent will have very little obli-
quity.

CHAP. LXXIV.—*Of a Figure moving against the
Wind,* Plate VIII.

A man moving against the wind in any direc-

tion, does not keep his centre of gravity duly disposed upon the centre of support*.

Chap. LXXV.—*Of the Balance of a Figure rest-ing upon its Feet.*

The man who rests upon his feet, either bears
the weight of his body upon them equally, or unequally. If equally, it will be with some accidental
weight, or simply with his own; if it be with an
additional weight, the opposite extremities of his
members will not be equally distant from the perpendicular of his feet. But if he simply carries
his own weight, the opposite extremities will be
equally distant from the perpendicular of his feet:
and on this subject of gravity I shall write a separate book†.

Chap. LXXVI.—*A Precept.*

The navel is always in the central or middle line
of the body, which passes through the pit of the
stomach to that of the neck, and must have as
much weight, either accidental or natural, on one
side of the human figure as on the other. This is
demonstrated by extending the arm, the wrist of
which performs the office of a weight at the end
of a steelyard; and will require some weight to be
thrown on the other side of the navel, to counter-

---

* See chap. lxiv.
† See in this work from chap. lx. to lxxxi.

balance that of the wrist. It is on that account
that the heel is often raised.

CHAP. LXXVII.—*Of a Man standing, but resting more upon one Foot than the other.*

After a man, by standing long, has tired the leg
upon which he rests, he sends part of his weight
upon the other leg. But this kind of posture is to
be employed only for old age, infancy, or extreme
lassitude, because it expresses weariness, or very
little power in the limbs. For that reason, a young
man, strong and healthy, will always rest upon
one of his legs, and if he removes a little of his
weight upon the other, it is only a necessary pre-
parative to motion, without which it is impossible
to move; as we have proved before, that motion
proceeds from inequality*.

CHAP. LXXVIII.—*Of the Balance of Figures,* Plate IX.

If the figure rests upon one foot, the shoulder
on that side will always be lower than the other;
and the pit of the neck will fall perpendicularly
over the middle of that leg which supports the
body. The same will happen in whatever other
view we see that figure, when it has not the arm
much extended, nor any weight on its back, in its

---

* See chapters lxi. lxiv.

c 5

hand, or on its shoulder, and when it does not, either behind or before, throw out that leg which does not support the body.

CHAP. LXXIX.—*In what Manner extending one Arm alters the Balance.*

THE extending of the arm, which was bent, removes the weight of the figure upon the foot which bears the weight of the whole body: as is observable in rope-dancers, who dance upon the rope with their arms open, without any pole.

CHAP. LXXX.—*Of a man bearing a weight on his Shoulders,* Plate X.

THE shoulder which bears the weight is always higher than the other. This is seen in the figure opposite, in which the centre line passes through the whole, with an equal weight on each side, to the leg on which it rests. If the weight were not equally divided on each side of this central line of gravity, the whole would fall to the ground. But Nature has provided, that as much of the natural weight of the man should be thrown on one side, as of accidental weight on the other, to form a counterpoise. This is effected by the man's bending, and leaning on the side not loaded, so as to form an equilibrium to the accidental weight he carries; and this cannot be done, unless the loaded shoulder be raised, and the other lowered. This is the resource

with which Nature has furnished a man on such
occasions.

Chap. LXXXI.—*Of Equilibrium.*

Any figure bearing an additional weight out of
the central line, must throw as much natural or accidental weight on the opposite side as is sufficient
to form a counterpoise round that line, which passes
from the pit of the neck, through the whole mass
of weight, to that part of the foot which rests upon
the ground.   We observe, that when a man lifts
a weight with one arm, he naturally throws out
the opposite arm ; and if that be not enough to
form an equipoise, he will add as much of his own
weight, by bending his body, as will enable him to
resist such accidental load.   We see also, that a
man ready to fall sideways and backwards at the
same time, always throws out the arm on the
opposite side.

Chap. LXXXII.—*Of Motion.*

Whether a man moves with velocity or slowness, the parts above the leg which sustains the
weight, will always be lower than the others on
the opposite side.

Chap. LXXXIII.—*The Level of the Shoulders.*

The shoulders or sides of a man, or any other
animal, will preserve less of their level, in proportion to the slowness of their motion ; and *vice*

versâ, those parts will lose less of their level when the motion is quicker. This is proved by the ninth proposition, treating of local motions, where it is said, any weight will press in the direction of the line of its motion; therefore the whole moving towards any one point, the parts belonging to it will follow the shortest line of the motion of its whole, without giving any of its weight to the collateral parts of the whole.

CHAP. LXXXIV.—*Objection to the above answered,* Plates XI. and XII.

It has been objected, in regard to the first part of the above proposition, that it does not follow that a man standing still, or moving slowly, has his members always in perfect balance upon the centre of gravity; because we do not find that Nature always follows that rule, but, on the contrary, the figure will sometimes bend sideways, standing upon one foot; sometimes it will rest part of its weight upon that leg which is bent at the knee, as is seen in the figures B. C.   But I shall reply thus, that what is not performed by the shoulders in the figure C, is done by the hip, as is demonstrated in another place.

CHAP. LXXXV.—*Of the Position of Figures,* Plate XIII.

In the same proportion as that part of the naked figure marked D A, lessens in height from

the shoulder to the hip, on account of its position
the opposite side increases. And this is the reason:
the figure resting upon one (suppose the left) foot,
that foot becomes the centre of all the weight above;
and the pit of the neck, formed by the junction of
the two clavicles, quits also its natural situation
at the upper extremity of the perpendicular line
(which passes through the middle surface of the
body), to bend over the same foot; and as this
line bends with it, it forces the transverse lines,
which are always at right angles, to lower their
extremities on that side where the foot rests, as
appears in A B C. The navel and middle parts
always preserve their natural height.

CHAP. LXXXVI.—*Of the Joints.*

In the bending of the joints it is particularly
useful to observe the difference and variety of
shape they assume; how the muscles swell on one
side, while they flatten on the other; and this is
more apparent in the neck, because the motion of
it is of three sorts, two of which are simple motions, and the other complex, participating also of
the other two.

The simple motions are, first, when the neck
bends towards the shoulder, either to the right or
left, and when it raises or lowers the head. The
second is, when it twists to the right or left, without rising or bending, but straight, with the head
turned towards one of the shoulders. The third

motion, which is called complex, is, when to the bending of it is added the twisting, as when the ear leans towards one of the shoulders, the head turning the same way, and the face turned upwards.

CHAP. LXXXVII.—*Of the Shoulders.*

Of those which the shoulders can perform, simple motions are the principal, such as moving the arm upwards and downwards, backwards and forwards. Though one might almost call those motions infinite, for if the arm can trace a circle upon a wall, it will have performed all the motions belonging to the shoulders. Every continued quantity being divisible *ad infinitum,* and this circle being a continued quantity, produced by the motion of the arm going through every part of the circumference, it follows, that the motions of the shoulders may also be said to be infinite.

CHAP. LXXXVIII.—*Of the Motions of a Man.*

When you mean to represent a man removing a weight, consider that the motions are various, viz. either a simple motion, by bending himself to raise the weight from the ground upwards, or when he drags the weight after him, or pushes it before him, or pulls it down with a rope passing through a pulley. It is to be observed, that the weight of the man's body pulls the more in proportion as the centre of his gravity is removed from the centre of

his support. To this must be added the strength of
the effort that the legs and back make when they
are bent, to return to their natural straight situation.

A man never ascends or descends, nor walks at
all in any direction, without raising the heel of the
back foot.

CHAP. LXXXIX.—*Of the Disposition of Members preparing to act with great Force*, Plate XIV.

When a man prepares himself to strike a violent blow, he bends and twists his body as far as
he can to the side contrary to that which he
means to strike, and collecting all his strength, he
by a complex motion, returns and falls upon the
point he has in view.*

CHAP. XC.—*Of Throwing any Thing with Violence*, Plate XV.

A man throwing a dart, a stone, or any thing
else with violence, may be represented, chiefly,
two different ways; that is, he may be preparing
to do it, or the act may be already performed.
If you mean to place him in the act of preparation,
the inside of the foot upon which he rests will be
under the perpendicular line of the pit of the neck;
and if it be the right foot, the left shoulder will be
perpendicular over the toes of the same foot.

* See chapters civ. cliv.

Chap. XCI.—*On the Motion of driving any thing into or drawing it out of the Ground.*

He who wishes to pitch a pole into the ground, or draw one out of it, will raise the leg and bend the knee opposite to the arm which acts, in order to balance himself upon the foot that rests, without which he could neither drive in, nor pull out any thing.

Chap. XCII.—*Of forcible Motions*, Plate XVI.

Of the two arms, that will be most powerful in its effort, which, having been farthest removed from its natural situation, is assisted more strongly by the other parts to bring it to the place where it means to go.   As the man A, who moves the arm with a club E, and brings it to the opposite side B, assisted by the motion of the whole body.

Chap. XCIII.—*The Action of Jumping.*

Nature will of itself, and without any reasoning in the mind of a man going to jump, prompt him to raise his arms and shoulders by a sudden motion, together with a great part of his body, and to lift them up high, till the power of the effort subsides.   This impetuous motion is accompanied by an instantaneous extension of the body which had bent itself, like a spring or bow, along the back, the joints of the thighs, knees, and feet, and is let off obliquely, that is upwards and forwards;

so that the disposition of the body tending forwards and upwards, makes it describe a great arch
when it springs up, which increases the leap.

CHAP. XCIV.—*Of the three Motions in jumping
upwards.*

When a man jumps upwards, the motion of the
head is three times quicker than that of the heel,
before the extremity of the foot quits the ground,
and twice as quick as that of the hips; because
three angles are opened and extended at the same
time : the superior one is that formed by the body
at its joint with the thigh before, the second is at
the joint of the thighs and legs behind, and the
third is at the instep before.*

CHAP. XCV.—*Of the easy Motions of Members.*

In regard to the freedom and ease of motions, it

* The author here means to compare the different quickness of
the motion of the head and the heel, when employed in the same
action of jumping ; and he states the proportion of the former
to be three times that of the latter. The reason he gives for this
is in substance, that as the head has but one motion to make,
while in fact the lower part of the figure has three successive
operations to perform at the places he mentions, three times the
velocity, or, in other words, three times the degree of effort, is
necessary in the head, the prime mover, to give the power of in-
fluencing the other parts; and the rule deducible from this axiom
is, that where two different parts of the body concur in the same
action, and one of them has to perform one motion only, while
the other is to have several, the proportion of velocity or effort
in the former must be regulated by the number of operations
necessary in the latter.

is very necessary to observe, that when you mean
to represent a figure which has to turn itself a little round, the feet and all the other members are
not to move in the same direction as the head.
But you will divide that motion among four joints,
viz. the feet, the knees, the hips, and the neck.
If it rests upon the right leg, the left knee should
be a little bent inward, with its foot somewhat
raised outward.   The left shoulder should be
lower than the other, and the nape of the neck
turned on the same side as the outward ankle of
the left foot, and the left shoulder perpendicular
over the great toe of the right foot.   And take it
as a general maxim, that figures do not turn their
heads straight with the chest, Nature having for
our convenience formed the neck so as to turn
with ease on every side when the eyes want to
look round; and to this the other joints are in
some measure subservient.   If the figure be sitting, and the arms have some employment across
the body, the breast will turn over the joint of
the hip.

CHAP. XCVI.—*The greatest Twist which a Man
can make, in turning to look at himself behind.*
Plate XVII.

The greatest twist that the body can perform is
when the back of the heels and the front of the
face are seen at the same time.   It is not done
without difficulty, and is effected by bending the

leg and lowering the shoulder on that side towards which the head turns.   The cause of this
motion, and also which of the muscles move first
and which last, I shall explain in my treatise on
anatomy.*

CHAP. XCVII.—*Of turning the Leg without the
Thigh.*

It is impossible to turn the leg inwards or outwards without turning the thigh by the same motion, because the setting in of the bones at the
knee is such, that they have no motion but backwards and forwards, and no more than is necessary for walking or kneeling; never sideways, because the form of the bones at the joint of the
knee does not allow it.   If this joint had been
made pliable on all sides, as that of the shoulder,
or that of the thigh bone with the hip, a man
would have had his legs bent on each side as often
as backwards and forwards, and seldom or never
straight with the thigh.   Besides, this joint can
bend only one way, so that in walking it can never
go beyond the straight line of the leg; it bends
only forwards, for if it could bend backwards, a
man could never get up again upon his feet, if
once he were kneeling; as when he means to get
up from the kneeling posture (on both knees), he
gives the whole weight of his body to one of the

* It is explained in this work, or at least there is something
respecting it in the preceding chapter, and in chap. cli.

knees to support, unloading the other, which at
that time feels no other weight than its own, and
therefore is lifted up with ease, and rests his foot
flat upon the ground; then returning the whole
weight upon that foot, and leaning his hand upon
his knee, he at once extends the other arm, raises
his head, and straightening the thigh with the
body, he springs up, and rests upon the same
foot, while he brings up the other.

CHAP. XCVIII.—*Postures of Figures.*

Figures that are set in a fixed attitude, are nevertheless to have some contrast of parts. If one
arm come before, the other remains still or goes
behind. If the figure rest upon one leg, the
shoulder on that side will be lower than the other.
This is observed by artists of judgment, who
always take care to balance the figure well upon
its feet, for fear it should appear to fall. Because
by resting upon one foot, the other leg being a
little bent, does not support the body any more
than if it were dead; therefore it is necessary that
the parts above that leg should transfer the centre of their weight upon the leg which supports
the body.

CHAP. XCIX.—*Of the Gracefulness of the Members.*

The members are to be suited to the body in

graceful motions, expressive of the meaning which the figure is intended to convey. If it had to give the idea of genteel and agreeable carriage, the members must be slender and well turned, but not lean; the muscles very slightly marked, indicating in a soft manner such as must necessarily appear; the arms, particularly, pliant, and no member in a straight line with any other adjoining member. If it happen, on account of the motion of the figure, that the right hip be higher than the left, make the joint of the shoulder fall perpendicularly on the highest part of that hip; and let that right shoulder be lower than the left. The pit of the neck will always be perpendicular over the middle of the instep of the foot that supports the body. The leg that does not bear will have its knee a little lower than the other, and near the other leg.

In regard to the positions of the head and arms, they are infinite, and for that reason I shall not enter into any detailed rule concerning them; suffice it to say, that they are to be easy and free, graceful, and varied in their bendings, so that they may not appear stiff like pieces of wood.

CHAP. C.—*That it is impossible for any Memory to retain the Aspects and Changes of the Members.*

It is impossible that any memory can be able to

retain all the aspects or motions of any member of any animal whatever. This case we shall exemplify by the appearance of the hand. And because any continued quantity is divisible *ad infinitum*, the motion of the eye which looks at the hand, and moves from A to B, moves by a space A B, which is also a continued quantity, and consequently divisible *ad infinitum*, and in every part of the motion varies to its view the aspect and figure of the hand; and so it will do if it move round the whole circle. The same will the hand do which is raised in its motion, that is, it will pass over a space, which is a continued quantity.*

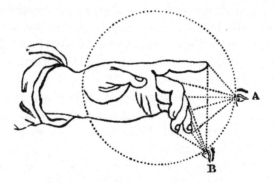

* The eyeball moving up and down to look at the hand, describes a part of a circle, from every point of which it sees it in an infinite variety of aspects. The hand also is moveable *ad infinitum* (for it can go round the whole circle—see chap. lxxxvii), and consequently shew itself in an infinite variety of aspects, which it is impossible for any memory to retain.

CHAP. CI.—*The Motions of Figures.*

Never put the head straight upon the shoulders, but a little turned sideways to the right or left, even though the figures should be looking up or down, or straight, because it is necessary to give them some motion of life and spirit. Nor ever compose a figure in such a manner, either in a front or back view, as that every part falls straight upon another from the top to the bottom. But if you wish to introduce such a figure, use it for old age. Never repeat the same motions of arms, or of legs, not only not in the same figure, but in those which are standing by, or near; if the necessity of the case, or the expression of the subject you represent, do not oblige you to it*.

CHAP. CII.—*Of common Motions.*

The variety of motions in man are equal to the variety of accidents or thoughts affecting the mind, and each of these thoughts, or accidents, will operate more or less, according to the temper and age of the subject; for the same cause will in the actions of youth, or of old age, produce very different effects.

CHAP. CIII.—*Of simple Motions.*

Simple motion is that which a man performs in merely bending backwards or forwards.

* See chap. xx. clv.

CHAP. CIV.—*Complex Motion.*

Complex motion is that which, to produce some particular action, requires the body to bend downwards and sideways at the same time. The painter must be careful in his compositions to apply these complex motions according to the nature of the subject, and not to weaken or destroy the effect of it by introducing figures with simple motions, without any connexion with the subject.

CHAP. CV.—*Motions appropriated to the Subject.*

The motions of your figures are to be expressive of the quantity of strength requisite to the force of the action. Let not the same effort be used to take up a stick as would easily raise a piece of timber. Therefore shew great variety in the expression of strength, according to the quality of the load to be managed.

CHAP. CVI.—*Appropriate Motions.*

There are some emotions of the mind which are not expressed by any particular motion of the body, while in others, the expression cannot be shewn without it. In the first, the arms fall down, the hands and all the other parts, which in general are the most active, remain at rest. But such emotions of the soul as produce bodily action, must put the members into such motions as are appropriated to the intention of the mind. This, however, is an ample subject, and we have a great deal to say upon it. There is a third kind of motion, which participates of the two already described; and a fourth, which depends neither on the one nor the other. This last belongs to insensibility, or fury, and should be ranked with madness or stupidity; and so adapted only to grotesque or Moresco work.

CHAP. CVII.—*Of the Postures of Women and young People.*

It is not becoming in women and young people to have their legs too much asunder, because it denotes boldness; while the legs close together shew modesty.

CHAP. CVIII.—*Of the Postures of Children.*

Children and old people are not to express quick motions, in what concerns their legs.

CHAP. CIX.—*Of the Motion of the Members.*

Let every member be employed in performing its proper functions. For instance, in a dead body, or one asleep, no member should appear alive or awake. A foot bearing the weight of the whole body, should not be playing its toes up and down, but flat upon the ground; except when it rests entirely upon the heel.

D

CHAP. CX.—*Of mental Motions.*

A mere thought, or operation of the mind, excites only simple and easy motions of the body; not this way, and that way, because its object is in the mind, which does not affect the senses when it is collected within itself.

CHAP. CXI.—*Effect of the Mind upon the Motions of the Body, occasioned by some outward Object.*

When the motion is produced by the presence of some object, either the cause is immediate or not. If it be immediate, the figure will first turn towards it the organs most necessary, the eyes; leaving its feet in the same place; and will only move the thighs, hips, and knees a little towards the same side, to which the eyes are directed.

LINEAR PERSPECTIVE.

CHAP. CXII.—*Of those who apply themselves to the Practice, without having learnt the Theory of the Art.*

Those who become enamoured of the practice of the art, without having previously applied to the diligent study of the scientific part of it, may be compared to mariners, who put to sea in a ship without rudder or compass, and therefore cannot be certain of arriving at the wished-for port.

Practice must always be founded on good theory; to this, Perspective is the guide and entrance, without which nothing can be well done.

CHAP. CXIII.—*Precepts in Painting.*

PERSPECTIVE is to Painting what the bridle is to a horse, and the rudder to a ship.

The size of a figure should denote the distance at which it is situated.

If a figure be seen of the natural size, remember that it denotes its being near to the eye.

CHAP. CXIV.—*Of the Boundaries of Objects, called Outlines or Contours.*

The outlines or contours of bodies are so little perceivable, that at any small distance between that and the object, the eye will not be able to recognize the features of a friend or relation, if it were not for their clothes and general appearance. So that by the knowledge of the whole it comes to know the parts.

CHAP. CXV.—*Of linear Perspective.*

LINEAR Perspective consists in giving, by

established rules, the true dimensions of objects, according to their respective distances; so that the second object be less than the first, the third than the second, and by degrees at last they become invisible. I find by experience, that, if the second object be at the same distance from the first, as the first is from the eye, though they be of the same size, the second will appear half the size of the first; and, if the third be at the same distance behind the second, it will diminish two thirds; and so on, by degrees, they will, at equal distances, diminish in proportion; provided that the interval be not more than twenty cubits *; at which distance it will lose two fourths of its size; at forty it will diminish three fourths; and at sixty it will lose five sixths, and so on progressively. But you must be distant from your picture twice the size of it; for, if you be only once the size, it will make a great difference in the measure from the first to the second.

CHAP. CXVI.—*What Parts of Objects disappear first by Distance.*

. .Those parts which are of less magnitude will first vanish from the sight †. This happens, be-

---

.* About thirteen yards of our measure; the Florentine braccia, or cubit, by which the author measures, being 1 foot 10 inches 7-8ths English measure.
. † See chap. cxxi. and cccv.

cause the shape of small objects, at an equal distance, comes to the eye under a more acute angle than the large ones, and the perception is less, in proportion as they are less in magnitude. It follows then, that if the large objects, by being removed to a great distance, and consequently coming to the eye by a small angle, are almost lost to the sight, the small objects will entirely disappear.

CXVII.—*Of remote Objects.*

The outlines of objects will be less seen, in proportion as they are more distant from the eye.

CHAP. CXVIII.—*Of the Point of Sight.*

The point of sight must be on a level with the eyes of a common-sized man, and placed upon the horizon, which is the line formed by a flat country terminating with the sky. An exception must be made as to mountains, which are above that line.

CHAP. CXIX.—*A Picture is to be viewed from one Point only.*

This will be proved by one single example. If you mean to represent a round ball very high up, on a flat and perpendicular wall, it will be necessary to make it oblong, like the shape of an egg, and to place yourself (that is, the eye, or point of view) so far back, as that its outline or circumference may appear round.

CHAP. CXX.—*Of the Dimensions of the first Figure in an historical Painting.*

The first figure in your picture will be less than Nature, in proportion as it recedes from the front of the picture, or the bottom line; and by the same rule the others behind it will go on lessening in an equal degree.*

CHAP. CXXI.—*Of Objects that are lost to the Sight in Proportion to their Distance.*

The first things that disappear, by being removed to some distance, are the outlines or boundaries of objects. The second, as they remove farther, are the shadows which divide contiguous bodies. The third are the thickness of legs and feet; and so in succession the small parts are lost to the sight, till nothing remains but a confused mass, without any distinct parts.

---

* It is supposed that the figures are to appear of the natural size, and not bigger. In that case, the measure of the first, to be of the exact dimension, should have its feet resting upon the bottom line; but as you remove it from that, it should diminish.

No allusion is here intended to the distance at which a picture is to be placed from the eye.

CHAP. CXXII.—*Errors not so easily seen in small Objects as in large ones.*

Supposing this small object to represent a man, or any other animal, although the parts, by being so much diminished or reduced, cannot be executed with the same exactness of proportion, nor finished with the same accuracy, as if on a larger scale, yet on that very account the faults will be less conspicuous. For example, if you look at a man at the distance of two hundred yards, and with all due attention mean to form a judgment, whether he be handsome or ugly, deformed or well made, you will find that, with all your endeavours, you can hardly venture to decide. The reason is, that the man diminishes so much by the distance, that it is impossible to distinguish the parts minutely. If you wish to know by demonstration the diminution of the above figure, hold your finger up before your eye at about nine inches distance, so that the top of your finger corresponds with the top of the head of the distant figure: you will perceive that your finger covers, not only its head, but part of its body; which is an evident proof of the apparent diminution of that object. Hence it often happens, that we are doubtful, and can scarcely, at some distance, distinguish the form of even a friend.

CHAP. CXXIII.—*Historical Subjects one above another on the same Wall to be avoided.*

This custom, which has been generally adopted by painters, on the front and sides of chapels, is much to be condemned. They begin with an historical picture, its landscape and buildings, in one compartment. After which, they raise another compartment, and execute another history with other buildings upon another level; and from thence they proceed to a third and fourth, varying the point of sight, as if the beholder was going up steps, while, in fact, he must look at them all from below, which is very ill-judged in those matters.

We know that the point of sight is the eye of the spectator; and if you ask, how is a series of subjects, such as the life of a saint, to be represented, in different compartments on the same wall? I answer, that you are to place the principal event in the largest compartment, and make the point of sight as high as the eye of the spectator. Begin that subject with large figures; and as you go up, lessen the objects, as well the figures, as buildings, varying the plans according to the effect of perspective; but never varying the point of sight: and so complete the series of subjects, till you come to a certain height, where terrestrial objects can be seen no more, except

the tops of trees, or clouds and birds; or if you
introduce figures, they must be aërial, such as
angels, or saints in glory, or the like, if they suit
the purpose of your history. If not, do not
undertake this kind of painting, for your work
will be faulty, and justly reprehensible.*

CHAP. CXXIV.—*Why Objects in Painting can
never detach, as natural Objects do.*

Painters often despair of being able to imitate
Nature, from observing, that their pictures have
not the same relief, nor the same life, as natural
objects have in a looking glass, though they both
appear upon a plain surface. They say, they have
colours which surpass in brightness the quality
of the lights, and in darkness the quality of the
shades of the objects seen in the looking-glass;
but attribute this circumstance to their own ignorance, and not to the true cause, because they do
not know it. It is impossible that objects in

* The author does not mean here to say, that one historical
picture cannot be hung over another. It certainly may, because, in viewing each, the spectator is at liberty (especially if
they are subjects independent of each other) to shift his place so
as to stand at the true point of sight for viewing every one of
them; but in covering a wall with a succession of subjects from
the same history, the author considers the whole as in fact but
one picture, divided into compartments, and to be seen at one
view, and which cannot therefore admit more than one point of
sight. In the former case the pictures are, in fact, so many distinct subjects unconnected with each other.

painting should appear with the same relief as those in the looking-glass, unless we look at them with only one eye.

The reason is this. The two eyes A B looking at objects one behind another, as M and N, see them both : because M cannot entirely occupy the space of N, by reason that the base of the visual rays is so broad, that the second object is seen behind the first. But if one eye be shut, and you look with the other S, the body F will entirely cover the body R, because the visual rays beginning at one point, form a triangle, of which the body F is the base, and being prolonged, they form two diverging tangents at the two extremities of F, which cannot touch the body R behind it, therefore can never see it.*

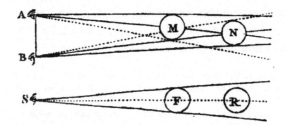

* See chap. cccxlviii.

This chapter is obscure, and may probably be made clear by merely stating it in other words. Leonardo objects to the use of both eyes, because, in viewing in that manner the objects here mentioned, two balls, one behind the other, the second is seen, ,

CHAP. CXXV.—*How to give the proper Dimension to Objects in Painting.*

In order to give the appearance of the natural size, if the piece be small (as miniatures), the

which would not be the case, if the angle of the visual rays were not too big for the first object. Whoever is at all acquainted with optics, need not be told, that the visual rays commence in a single point in the centre, or nearly the centre of each eye, and continue diverging. But, in using both eyes, the visual rays proceed not from one and the same centre, but from a different centre in each eye, and intersecting each other, as they do a a little before passing the first object, they become together broader than the extent of the first object, and consequently give a view of part of the second. On the contrary, in using but one eye, the visual rays proceed but from one centre; and as, therefore, there cannot be any intersection, the visual rays, when they reach the first object, are not broader than the first object, and the second is completely hidden. Properly speaking, therefore, in using both eyes we introduce more than one point of sight, which renders the perspective false in the painting; but in using one eye only, there can be, as there ought, but one point of sight. There is, however, this difference between viewing real objects and those represented in painting, that in looking at the former, whether we use one or both eyes, the objects, by being actually detached from the back ground, admit the visual rays to strike on them, so as to form a correct perspective, from whatever point they are viewed, and the eye accordingly forms a perspective of its own; but in viewing the latter, there is no possibility of varying the perspective; and, unless the picture is seen precisely under the same angle as it was painted under, the perspective in all other views must be false. This is observable in the perspective views painted for scenes at the playhouse. If the beholder is seated in the central line of the house, whether in the boxes or pit, the perspective is correct; but, in proportion as he is placed at a greater or less distance to the right or left of that line, the perspective appears to him more or less faulty. And hence arises the necessity of using but one eye in viewing a painting, in order thereby to reduce it to one point of sight.

figures on the fore-ground are to be finished with
as much precision as those of any large painting,
because being small they are to be brought up
close to the eye. But large paintings are seen at
some distance; whence it happens, that though
the figures in each are so different in size, in appearance they will be the same. This proceeds
from the eye receiving those objects under the
same angle; and it is proved thus. Let the large

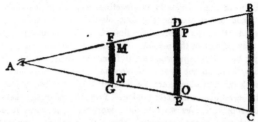

painting be B C, the eye A, and D E a pane of
glass, through which are seen the figures situated
at B C. I say that the eye being fixed, the figures
in the copy of the paintings B C are to be smaller,
in proportion as the glass D E is nearer the eye A,
and are to be as precise and finished. But if you
will execute the picture B C upon the glass D E,
this ought to be less finished than the picture B
C, and more so than the figure M N transferred
upon the glass F G; because, supposing the figure
P O to be as much finished as the natural one in
B C, the perspective of O P would be false, since,
though in regard to the diminution of the figure

it would be right, B C being diminished in P O, finishing would not agree with the distance, because in giving it the perfection of the natural B C, B C would appear as near as O P; but, if you search for the diminution of O P, O P will be found at the distance B C, and the diminution of the finishing as at F G.

CHAP. CXXVI.—*How to draw accurately any particular Spot.*

Take a glass as large as your paper, fasten it well between your eye and the object you mean to draw, and fixing your head in a frame (in such a manner as not to be able to move it) at the distance of two feet from the glass; shut one eye, and draw with a pencil accurately upon the glass all that you see through it. After that, trace upon paper what you have drawn on the glass, which tracing you may paint at pleasure, observing the aerial perspective.

CHAP. CXXVII.—*Disproportion to be avoided, even in the accessory Parts.*

A great fault is committed by many painters, which is highly to be blamed, that is, to represent the habitations of men, and other parts of their compositions, so low, that the doors do not reach as high as the knees of their inhabitants, though, according to their situation, they are nearer to the

eye of the spectator, than the men who seem
willing to enter them. I have seen some pictures
with porticos, supported by columns loaded with
figures; one grasping a column against which it
leans, as if it were a walking stick, and other similar errors, which are to be avoided with the greatest
care.

INVENTION, or COMPOSITION.

CHAP. CXXVIII.—*Precept for avoiding a bad Choice in the Style or Proportion of Figures.*

THE painter ought to form his style upon the most proportionate model in Nature; and after having measured that, he ought to measure himself also, and be perfectly acquainted with his own defects or deficiencies; and having acquired this knowledge, his constant care should be to avoid conveying into his work those defects which he has found in his own person; for these defects, becoming habitual to his observation, mislead his judgment, and he perceives them no longer. We ought, therefore, to struggle against such a prejudice, which grows up with us; for the mind, being fond of its own habitation, is apt to represent it to our imagination as beautiful. From the same motive it may be, that there is not a woman, however plain in her person, who may not find her admirer, if she be not a monster. Against this bent of the mind you ought very cautiously to be on your guard.

CHAP. CXXIX.—*Variety in Figures..*

A painter ought to aim at universal excellence; for he will be greatly wanting in dignity, if he do one thing well and another badly, as many do, who study only the naked figure, measured and proportioned by a pair of compasses in their hands, and do not seek for variety. A man may be well proportioned, and yet be tall or short, large or lean, or of a middle size ; and whoever does not make great use of these varieties, which are all existing in Nature in its most perfect state, will produce figures as if cast in one and the same mould, which is highly reprehensible.

CHAP. CXXX.—*How a Painter ought to proceed in his Studies.*

The painter ought always to form in his mind a kind of system of reasoning or discussion within himself on any remarkable object before him. He should stop, take notes, and form some rule upon it ; considering the place, the circumstances, the lights and shadows.

CHAP. CXXXI.—*Of sketching Histories and Figures.*

Sketches of historical subjects must be slight, attending only to the situation of the figures, without regard to the finishing of particular members, which may be done afterwards at leisure, when the mind is so disposed.

CHAP. CXXXII.—*How to study Composition.*

The young student should begin by sketching slightly some single figure, and turn that on all sides, knowing already how to contract, and how to

extend the members; after which, he may put two
together in various attitudes, we will suppose in the
act of fighting boldly.   This composition also he
must try on all sides, and in a variety of ways,
tending to the same expression.   Then he may
imagine one of them very courageous, while the
other is a coward.   Let these attitudes, and many
other accidental affections of the mind, be with
great care studied, examined, and dwelt upon.

CHAP. CXXXIII.—*Of the Attitudes of Men.*

The attitudes and all the members are to be
disposed in such a manner, that by them the intentions of the mind may be easily discovered.

CHAP. CXXXIV.—*Variety of Positions.*

The positions of the human figure are to be
adapted to the age and rank; and to be varied according to the difference of the sexes, men or
women.

CHAP. CXXXV.—*Of Studies from Nature for
History.*

It is necessary to consider well the situation for
which the history is to be painted, particularly the
height; and let the painter place accordingly the
model from which he means to make his studies
for that historical picture; and set himself as much
below the object, as the picture is to be above the
eye of the spectator, otherwise the work will be
faulty.

CHAP. CXXXVI.—*Of the Variety of Figures in History Painting.*

History painting must exhibit variety in its fullest extent. In temper, size, complexion, actions, plumpness, leanness, thick, thin, large, small, rough, smooth, old age and youth, strong and muscular, weak, with little appearance of muscles, cheerfulness, and melancholy. Some should be with curled hair, and some with straight; some short, some long, some quick in their motions, and some slow, with a variety of dresses and colours, according as the subject may require.

CHAP. CXXXVII.—*Of Variety in History.*

A painter should delight in introducing great variety into his compositions, avoiding repetition, that by this fertility of invention he may attract and charm the eye of the beholder. If it be requisite, according to the subject meant to be represented, that there should be a mixture of men differing in their faces, ages, and dress, grouped with women, children, dogs, and horses, buildings, hills and flat country; observe dignity and decorum in the principal figure; such as a king, magistrate, or philosopher, separating them from the low classes of the people. Mix not afflicted or weeping figures with joyful and laughing ones; for Nature dictates that the cheerful be attended by others of the same disposition of mind. Laughter is productive of laughter, and *vice versâ*.

Chap. CXXXVIII.—*Of the Age of Figures.*

Do not bring together a number of boys with as many old men, nor young men with infants, nor women with men; if the subject you mean to represent does not oblige you to it.

Chap. CXXXIX.—*Of Variety of Faces.*

The Italian painters have been accused of a common fault, that is, of introducing into their compositions the faces, and even the whole figures, of Roman emperors, which they take from the antique. To avoid such an error, let no repetition take place, either in parts, or the whole of a figure; nor let there be even the same face in another composition; and the more the figures are contrasted, viz. the deformed opposed to the beautiful, the old to the young, the strong to the feeble, the more the picture will please and be admired. These different characters, contrasted with each other, will increase the beauty of the whole.

It frequently happens that a painter, while he is composing, will use any little sketch or scrap of drawing he has by him, and endeavour to make it serve his purpose; but this is extremely injudicious, because he may very often find that the

members he has drawn have not the motion suited
to what he means to express; and after he has
adopted, accurately drawn, and even well finished
them, he will be loth to rub out and change them
for others.

CHAP. CXL.—*A Fault in Painters.*

It is a very great fault in a painter to repeat the
same motions in figures, and the same folds in
draperies in the same composition, as also to
make all the faces alike.

CHAP. CXLI.—*How you may learn to compose
Groups for History Painting.*

When you are well instructed in perspective,
and know perfectly how to draw the anatomy and
forms of different bodies or objects, it should be
your delight to observe and consider in your
walks the different actions of men, when they are
talking, or quarrelling; when they laugh, and when
they fight. Attend to their positions, and to those
of the spectators; whether they are attempting to
separate those who fight, or merely lookers-on.
Be quick in sketching these with slight strokes in
your pocket-book, which should always be about
you, and made of stained paper, as you ought not
to rub out. When it is full, take another, for
these are not things to be rubbed out, but kept
with the greatest care; because forms and mo-

tions of bodies are so infinitely various, that the memory is not able to retain them; therefore preserve these sketches as your assistants and masters.

CHAP. CXLII.—*How to study the Motions of the human Body.*

The first requisite towards a perfect acquaintance with the various motions of the human body, is the knowledge of all the parts, particularly the joints, in all the attitudes in which it may be placed. Then make slight sketches in your pocketbook as opportunities occur, of the actions of men, as they happen to meet your eye, without being perceived by them; because, if they were to observe you, they would be disturbed from that freedom of action, which is prompted by inward feeling; as when two men are quarrelling and angry, each of them seeming to be in the right, and with great vehemence move their eyebrows, arms, and all the other members, using motions appropriated to their words and feelings. This they could not do, if you wanted them to imitate anger, or any other accidental emotion; such as laughter, weeping, pain, admiration, fear, and the like. For that reason, take care never to be without a little book, for the purpose of sketching those various motions, and also groups of people standing by. This will teach you how to compose

history. Two things demand the principal attention of a good painter. One is the exact outline
and shape of the figure ; the other, the true expression of what passes in the mind of that figure,
which he must feel, and that is very important.

CHAP. CXLIII.—*Of Dresses, and of Draperies
and Folds.*

The draperies with which you dress figures
ought to have their folds so accommodated as to
surround the parts they are intended to cover ;
that in the mass of light there be not any dark
fold, and in the mass of shadows none receiving
too great a light. They must go gently over,
describing the parts ; but not with lines across,
cutting the members with hard notches, deeper
than the part can possibly be ; at the same time,
it must fit the body, and not appear like an empty
bundle of cloth ; a fault of many painters, who,
enamoured of the quantity and variety of folds,
have encumbered their figures, forgetting the intention of clothes, which is to dress and surround
the parts gracefully wherever they touch ; and
not to be filled with wind, like bladders puffed up
where the parts project. I do not deny that we
ought not to neglect introducing some handsome
folds among these draperies, but it must be done
with great judgment, and suited to the parts,
where, by the actions of the limbs and position of

the whole body, they gather together.   Above all, be careful to vary the quality and quantity of your folds in compositions of many figures; so that, if some have large folds, produced by thick woollen cloth, others, being dressed in thinner stuff, may have them narrower; some sharp and straight, others soft and undulating.

CHAP. CXLIV.—*Of the Nature of Folds in Draperies.*

Many painters prefer making the folds of their draperies with acute angles, deep and precise; others with angles hardly perceptible; and some with none at all; but instead of them, certain curved lines.

CHAP. CXLV.—*How the Folds of Draperies ought to be represented,* Plate XVIII.

That part of the drapery, which is the farthest from the place where it is gathered, will appear more approaching its natural state.   Every thing naturally inclines to preserve its primitive form. Therefore a stuff or cloth, which is of equal thickness on both sides, will always incline to remain flat.   For that reason, when it is constrained by some fold to relinquish its flat situation, it is observed that, at the part of its greatest restraint, it is continually making efforts to return to its natural shape; and the parts most distant from it re-assume more of their primitive state by ample and distended folds. For example, let A B C be the drapery mentioned above; A B the place where it is folded or restrained. I have said that the part, which is farthest from the place of its restraint, would return more toward its primitive shape. Therefore C being the farthest, will be broader and more extended than any other part.

CHAP. CXLVI.—*How the Folds in Draperies ought to be made.*

Draperies are not to be encumbered with many folds: on the contrary, there ought to be some only where they are held up with the hands or arms of the figures, and the rest left to fall with natural simplicity. They ought to be studied from nature; that is to say, if a woollen cloth be intended, the folds ought to be drawn after such cloth; if it be of silk, or thin stuff, or else very thick for labourers, let it be distinguished by the nature of the folds. But never copy them, as some do, after models dressed in paper, or thin leather, for it greatly misleads.

CHAP. CXLVII.—*Fore-shortening of Folds,* Plate XIX.

Where the figure is fore-shortened, there ought to appear a greater number of folds, than on the other parts, all surrounding it in a circular man-

ner. Let E be the situation of the eye. M N
will have the middle of every circular fold successively removed farther from its outline, in
proportion as it is more distant from the eye. In
M O of the other figure the outlines of these
circular folds will appear almost straight, because
it is situated opposite the eye; but in P and Q
quite the contrary, as in N and M.

Chap. CXLVIII.—*Of Folds.*

The folds of draperies, whatever be the motion
of the figure, ought always to shew, by the form
of their outlines, the attitude of such figure; so
as to leave, in the mind of the beholder, no
doubt or confusion in regard to the true position
of the body; and let there be no fold, which, by
its shadow, breaks through any of the members;
that is to say, appearing to go in deeper than the
surface of the part it covers. And if you represent the figure clothed with several garments, one
over the other, let it not appear as if the upper
one covered only a mere skeleton; but let it express that it is also well furnished with flesh, and
a thickness of folds, suitable to the number of
its under garments.

The folds surrounding the members ought to
diminish in thickness near the extremities of the
part they surround.

The length of the folds, which are close to the

E

members, ought to produce other folds on that side where the member is diminished by foreshortening, and be more extended on the opposite side.

CHAP. CXLIX.—*Of Decorum.*

Observe decorum in every thing you represent, that is, fitness of action, dress, and situation, according to the dignity or meanness of the subject to be represented. Be careful that a king, for instance, be grave and majestic in his countenance and dress; that the place be well decorated; and that his attendants, or the by-standers, express reverence and admiration, and appear as noble, in dresses suitable to a royal court.

On the contrary, in the representation of a mean subject, let the figures appear low and despicable; those about them with similar countenances and actions, denoting base and presumptuous minds, and meanly clad. In short, in both cases, the parts must correspond with the general sentiment of the composition.

The motions of old age should not be similar to those of youth; those of a woman to those of a man; nor should the latter be the same as those of a boy.

CHAP. CL.—*The Character of Figures in Composition.*

In general, the painter ought to introduce very

few old men, in the ordinary course of historical
subjects, and those few separated from young
people; because old people are few, and their
habits do not agree with those of youth. Where
there is no conformity of custom, there can be
no intimacy, and, without it, a company is soon
separated. But if the subject require an appearance of gravity, a meeting on important business,
as a council, for instance, let there be few young
men introduced, for youth willingly avoids such
meetings.

CHAP. CLI.—*The Motion of the Muscles, when
the Figures are in natural Positions.*

A figure, which does not express by its position
the sentiments and passions, by which we suppose it animated, will appear to indicate that its
muscles are not obedient to its will, and the
painter very deficient in judgment. For that reason, a figure is to shew great eagerness and meaning; and its position is to be so well appropriated
to that meaning, that it cannot be mistaken, nor
made use of for any other.

CHAP. CLII.—*A Precept in Painting.*

The painter ought to notice those quick motions, which men are apt to make without thinking, when impelled by strong and powerful affections of the mind. He ought to take memoran-

E 2

dums of them, and sketch them in his pocket-book, in order to make use of them when they may answer his purpose; and then to put a living model in the same position, to see the quality and aspect of the muscles which are in action.

CHAP. CLIII.—*Of the Motion of Man,* Plates XX. and XXI.

The first and principal part of the art is composition of any sort, or putting things together. The second relates to the expression and motion of the figures, and requires that they be well appropriated, and seeming attentive to what they are about; appearing to move with alacrity and spirit, according to the degree of expression suitable to the occasion; expressing slow and tardy motions, as well as those of eagerness in pursuit: and that quickness and ferocity be expressed with such force as to give an idea of the sensations of the actors. When a figure is to throw a dart, stones, or the like, let it be seen evidently by the attitude and disposition of all the members, that such is its intention; of which there are two two examples in the opposite plates, varied both in action and power. The first in point of vigour is A. The second is B. But A will throw his weapon farther than B, because, though they seem desirous of throwing it to the same point, A having turned his feet towards the object, while

his body is twisted and bent back the contrary
way, to increase his power, returns with more
velocity and force to the point to which he means
to throw.   But the figure B having turned his
feet the same way as his body, it returns to its
place with great inconvenience, and consequently
with weakened powers.   For in the expression of
great efforts, the preparatory motions of the
body must be strong and violent, twisting and
bending, so that it may return with convenient
ease, and by that means have a great effect.   In
the same manner, if a cross-bow be not strung
with force, the motion of whatever it shoots will
be short and without effect; because, where
there is no impulse, there can be no motion; and
if the impulse be not violent, the motion is but
tardy and feeble.   So a bow which is not strung
has no motion; and if it be strung, it will remain
in that state till the impulse be given by another power which puts it in motion, and it
will shoot with a violence equal to that which
was employed in bending it.   In the same
manner, the man who does not twist and
bend his body will have acquired no power.
Therefore, after A has thrown his dart, he will
find himself twisted the contrary way, viz. on the
side where he. has thrown; and he will have
acquired only power sufficient to serve him to
return to where he was at first.

CHAP. CLIV.—*Of Attitudes and the Motions of the Members.*

The same attitude is not to be repeated in the same picture, nor the same motion of members in the same figure, nay, not even in the hands or fingers.

And if the history requires a great number of figures, such as a battle, or a massacre of soldiers, in which there are but three ways of striking, viz. thrusting, cutting, or back-handed; in that case you must take care, that all those who are cutting be expressed in different views; some turning their backs, some their sides, and others be seen in front; varying in the same manner the three different ways of fighting, so that all the actions may have a relation to those three principles. In battles, complex motions display great art, giving spirit and animation to the whole. By complex motion is meant, for instance, that of a single figure shewing the front of the legs, and the same time the profile of the shoulder. But of this I shall treat in another place.*

CHAP. CLV.—*Of a single Figure separate from an historical Group.*

The same motion of members should not be re-

* Chap. xcvi. and civ.

peated in a figure which you mean to be alone; for instance, if the figure be represented running it must not throw both hands forward; but one forward and the other backward, or else it cannot run. If the right foot come forward, the right arm must go backward and the left forward, because, without such disposition and contrast of parts, it is impossible to run well. If another figure be supposed to follow this, one of its legs should be brought somewhat forward, and the other be perpendicular under the head; the arm on the same side should pass forward. But of this we shall treat more fully in the book on motion. *

CHAP. CLVI.— *On the Attitudes of the human Figure.*

A painter is to be attentive to the motions and actions of men, occasioned by some sudden accident. He must observe them on the spot, take sketches, and not wait till he wants such expression, and then have it counterfeited for him; for instance, setting a model to weep when there is no cause; such an expression without a cause will be neither quick nor natural. But it will be of great use to have observed every action from nature, as it

---

* See the Life of the Author chap. xx. and ci. of the present work.

occurs, and then to have a model set in the same
attitude to help the recollection, and find out
something to the purpose, according to the subject
in hand.

CHAP. CLVII.—*How to represent a Storm.*

To form a just idea of a storm, you must consider it attentively in its effects. When the wind
blows violently over the sea or land, it removes
and carries off with it everything that is not firmly
fixed to the general mass. The clouds must
appear straggling and broken, carried according to
the direction and the force of the wind, and
blended with clouds of dust raised from the sandy
shore. Branches and leaves of trees must be
represented as carried along by the violence of the
storm, and together with numberless other light
substances, scattered in the air. Trees and grass
must be bent to the ground, as if yielding to the
course of the wind. Boughs must be twisted out
of their natural form, with their leaves reversed
and entangled. Of the figures dispersed in the picture, some should appear thrown on the ground, so
wrapped up in their cloaks and covered with dust,
as to be scarcely distinguishable. Of those who
remain on their feet, some should be sheltered by
and holding fast behind some great trees, to avoid
the same fate: others bending to the ground,
their hands over their faces to ward off the dust;

their hair and their clothes flying straight up at
the mercy of the wind.

The high tremendous waves of the stormy sea
will be covered with foaming froth; the most subtle parts of which, being raised by the wind, like
a thick mist, mix with the air.   What vessels are
seen should appear with broken cordage, and torn
sails, fluttering in the wind; some with broken
masts fallen across the hulk, already on its side
amidst the tempestuous waves.   Some of the crew
should be represented as if crying aloud for help,
and clinging to the remains of the shattered vessel.
Let the clouds appear as driven by tempestuous
winds against the summits of lofty mountains,
enveloping those mountains, and breaking and
recoiling with redoubled force, like waves against
a rocky shore.   The air should be rendered awfully
dark, by the mist, dust, and thick clouds.

CHAP. CLVIII.—*How to compose a battle.*

First, let the air exhibit a confused mixture of
smoke, arising from the discharge of artillery and
musquetry, and the dust raised by the horses of
the combatants; and observe, that dust being of
an earthy nature, is heavy; but yet, by reason of
its minute particles, it is easily impelled upwards,
and mixes with the air; nevertheless, it naturally
falls downwards again, the most subtle parts of it
alone gaining any considerable degree of elevation;

and at its utmost height it is so thin and transparent, as to appear nearly of the colour of the air. The smoke, thus mixing with the dusty air, forms a kind of dark cloud, at the top of which it is distinguished from the dust by a blueish cast, the dust retaining more of its natural colour. On that part from which the light proceeds, this mixture of air, smoke, and dust, will appear much brighter than on the opposite side. The more the combatants are involved in this turbulent mist, the less distinctly they will be seen, and the more confused will they be in their lights and shades. Let the faces of the musketeers, their bodies, and every object near them, be tinged with a reddish hue, even the air or cloud of dust; in short, all that surrounds them. This red tinge you will diminish, in proportion to their distance from the primary cause. The group of figures, which appear at a distance between the spectator and the light, will form a dark mass upon a light ground; and their legs will be more undetermined and lost as they approach nearer to the ground; because there the dust is heavier and thicker.

If you mean to represent some straggling horses running out of the main body, introduce also some small clouds of dust, as far distant from each other as the leap of the horse, and these little clouds will become fainter, more scanty, and dif_fused, in proportion to their distance from the horse. That nearest to his feet will consequently be the most determined, smallest, and the thickest of all.

Let the air be full of arrows, in all directions; some ascending, some falling down, and some darting straight forwards. The bullets of the musketry, though not seen, will be marked in their course by a train of smoke, which breaks through the general confusion. The figures in the foreground should have their hair covered with dust, as also their eyebrows; and all parts liable to receive it.

The victorious party will be running forwards, their hair and other light parts flying in the wind, their eyebrows lowered, and the motion of every member properly contrasted; for instance, in moving the right foot forwards, the left arm must be brought forward also. If you make any of them fallen down, mark the trace of his fall on the slippery, gore-stained dust; and where the ground is less impregnated with blood, let the print of men's feet and of horses, that have passed that way, be marked. Let there be some horses dragging the bodies of their riders, and leaving behind them a furrow, made by the body thus trailed along.

The countenances of the vanquished will appear pale and dejected. Their eyebrows raised, and much wrinkled about the forehead and cheeks.

The tip of their noses somewhat divided from the nostrils by arched wrinkles terminating at the corner of the eyes, those wrinkles being occasioned by the opening and raising of the nostrils; the upper lips turned up, discovering the teeth. Their mouths wide open, and expressive of violent lamentation. One may be seen fallen wounded on the ground, endeavouring with one hand to support his body, and covering his eyes with the other, the palm of which is turned towards the enemy. Others running away, and with open mouths seeming to cry aloud. Between the legs of the combatants let the ground be strewed with all sorts of arms; as broken shields, spears, swords, and the like. Many dead bodies should be introduced, some entirely covered with dust, others in part only; let the blood, which seems to issue immediately from the wound, appear of its natural colour, and running in a winding course, till, mixing with the dust, it forms a reddish kind of mud. Some should be in the agonies of death; their teeth shut, their eyes wildly staring, their fists clenched, and their legs in a distorted position. Some may appear disarmed, and beaten down by the enemy, still fighting with their fists and teeth, and endeavouring to take a passionate, though unavailing revenge. There may be also a straggling horse without a rider, running in wild disorder; his mane flying in the

wind, beating down with his feet all before him
and doing a deal of damage, A wounded soldier
may also be seen falling to the ground, and attempting to cover himself with his shield, while
an enemy bending over him endeavours to give
him the finishing stroke. Several dead bodies
should be heaped together under a dead horse.
Some of the conquerers, as having ceased fighting,
may be wiping their faces from the dirt, collected
on them by the mixture of dust with the water
from their eyes.

The *corps de reserve* will be seen advancing
gaily, but cautiously, their eyebrows directed forwards, shading their eyes with their hands to observe the motions of the enemy, amidst clouds of
dust and smoke, and seeming attentive to the
orders of their chief. You may also make their
commander holding up his staff, pushing forwards,
and pointing towards the place where they are
wanted. A river may likewise be introduced, with
horses fording it, dashing the water about between
their legs, and in the air, covering all the adjacent
ground with water and foam. Not a spot is to
be left without some marks of blood and carnage.

CHAP. CLIX.—*The Representation of an Orator
and his Audience.*

If you have to represent a man who is speaking
to a large assembly of people, you are to consider

the subject matter of his discourse, and to adapt
his attitude to such subject. If he means to persuade, let it be known by his gesture. If he is
giving an explanation, deduced from several reasons, let him put two fingers of the right hand
within one of the left, having the other two bent
close, his face turned towards the audience, with
the mouth half open, seeming to speak. If he is
sitting, let him appear as going to raise himself up
a little, and his head be forward. But if he is
represented standing, let him bend his chest and
his head forward towards the people.

The auditory are to appear silent and attentive,
with their eyes upon the speaker, in the act of
admiration. There should be some old men, with
their mouths close shut, in token of approbation,
and their lips pressed together, so as to form wrinkles at the corners of the mouth, and about the
cheeks, and forming others about the forehead, by
raising the eyebrows, as if struck with astonish-
ment. Some others of those sitting by, should be
seated with their hands within each other, round
one of their knees; some with one knee upon the
other, and upon that, one hand receiving the elbow,
the other supporting the chin, covered with a ve-
nerable beard.

CHAP. CLX.—*Of demonstrative Gestures.*

The action by which a figure points at any thing

near, either in regard to time or situation, is to be expressed by the hand very little removed from the body. But if the same thing is far distant, the hand must also be far removed from the body, and the face of the figure pointing, must be turned towards those to whom he is pointing it out.

CHAP. CLXI.—*Of the Attitudes of the By-standers at some remarkable Event.*

All those who are present at some event deserving notice, express their admiration, but in various manners. As when the hand of justice punishes some malefactor. If the subject be an act of devotion, the eyes of all present should be directed towards the object of their adoration, aided by a variety of pious actions with the other members; as at the elevation of the host at mass, and other similar ceremonies. If it be a laughable subject, or one exciting compassion and moving to tears, in those cases it will not be necessary for all to have their eyes turned towards the object, but they will express their feelings by different actions; and let there be several assembled in groups, to rejoice or lament together. If the event be terrific, let the faces of those who run away from the sight, be strongly expressive of fright, with various motions; as shall be described in the tract on Motion.

CHAP. CLXII.—*How to represent Night.*

Those objects which are entirely deprived of
light, are lost to the sight, as in the night; therefore if you mean to paint a history under those
circumstances, you must suppose a large fire, and
those objects that are near it to be tinged with its
colour, and the nearer they are the more they will
partake of it. The fire being red, all those objects
which receive light from it will appear of a reddish
colour, and those that are most distant from it
will partake of the darkness that surrounds them.
The figures which are represented before the fire
will appear dark in proportion to the brightness of
the fire, because those parts of them which we see,
are tinged by that darkness of the night, and not
by the light of the fire, which they intercept.
Those that are on either side of the fire, will be
half in the shade of night, and half in the red light.
Those seen beyond the extent of the flames, will
be all of a reddish light upon a black ground. In
regard to their attitudes, let those who are nearest
the fire, make screens of their hands and cloaks,
against the scorching heat, with their faces turned
on the contrary side, as if ready to run away from
it. The most remote will only be shading their
eyes with their hands, as if hurt by the too great
glare.

Chap. CLXIII.—*The Method of awakening the Mind to a Variety of Inventions.*

I will not omit to introduce among these precepts a new kind of speculative invention, which though apparently trifling, and almost laughable, is nevertheless of great utility in assisting the genius to find variety for composition.

By looking attentively at old and smeared walls, or stones and veined marble of various colours, you may fancy that you see in them several compositions, landscapes, battles, figures in quick motion, strange countenances, and dresses, with an infinity of other objects. By these confused lines the inventive genius is excited to new exertions.

Chap. CLXIV.—*Of Composition in History.*

When the painter has only a single figure to represent, he must avoid any shortening whatever, as well of any particular member, as of the whole figure, because he would have to contend with the prejudices of those who have no knowledge in that branch of the art. But in subjects of history, composed of many figures, shortenings may be introduced with great propriety, nay, they are indispensable, and ought to be used without reserve, as the subject may require; particularly in battles, where of course many shortenings and contortions of figures happen, amongst such an enraged multitude of actors, possessed, as it were, of a brutal madness.

EXPRESSION AND CHARACTER.

Chap. CLXV.—*Of expressive Motions.*

Let your figures have actions appropriated to what they are intended to think or say, and these will be well learnt by imitating the deaf, who by the motion of their hands, eyes, eyebrows, and the whole body, endeavour to express the sentiments of their mind. Do not ridicule the thought of a master without a tongue teaching you an art he does not understand; he will do it better by his expressive motions, than all the rest by their words and examples. Let then the painter, of whatever school, attend well to this maxim, and apply it to the different qualities of the figures he represents, and to the nature of the subject in which they are actors.

Chap. CLXVI.—*How to paint Children.*

Children are to be represented with quick and contorted motions, when they are sitting; but when standing, with fearful and timid motions.

CHAP. CLXVII.—*How to represent old Men.*

Old men must have slow and heavy motions; their legs and knees must be bent when they are standing, and their feet placed parallel and wide asunder. Let them be bowed downwards, the head leaning much forward, and their arms very little extended.

CHAP. CLXVIII.—*How to paint old Women.*

Old women, on the contrary, are to be represented bold and quick, with passionate motions, like furies*. But the motions are to appear a great deal quicker in their arms than in their legs.

CHAP. CLXIX.—*How to paint Women.*

Women are to be represented in modest and reserved attitudes, with their knees rather close, their arms drawing near each other, or folded about the body; their heads looking downwards, and leaning a little on one side.

CHAP. CLXX.—*Of the Variety of Faces.*

The countenances of your figures should be ex-

* The author here speaks of unpolished nature; and indeed it is from such subjects only, that the genuine and characteristic operations of nature are to be learnt. It is the effect of education to correct the natural peculiarities and defects, and, by so doing, to assimilate one person to the rest of the world.

pressive of their different situations: men at work, at rest, weeping, laughing, crying out, in fear, or joy, and the like. The attitudes also, and all the members, ought to correspond with the sentiment expressed in the faces.

CHAP. CLXXI.—*The Parts of the Face and their Motions.*

The motions of the different parts of the face, occasioned by sudden agitations of the mind, are many. The principal of these are Laughter, Weeping, Calling out, Singing, either in a high or low pitch, Admiration, Anger, Joy, Sadness, Fear, Pain, and others, of which I propose to treat. First, of Laughing and Weeping, which are very similar in the motion of the mouth, the cheeks, the shutting of the eyebrows, and the space between them; as we shall explain in its place, in treating of the changes which happen in the face, hands, fingers, and all the other parts of the body, as they are affected by the different emotions of the soul; the knowledge of which is absolutely necessary to a painter, or else his figures may be said to be twice dead. But it is very necessary also that he be careful not to fall into the contrary extreme; giving extraordinary motions to his figures, so that in a quiet and peaceable subject, he does not seem to represent a battle, or the revellings of drunken men: but, above all, the actors in any point of history must be attentive to what they are about, or to what is going forward; with actions that denote admiration, respect, pain, suspicion, fear, and joy, according as the occasion, for which they are brought together, may require. Endeavour that different points of history be not placed one above the other on the same canvass, nor walls with different horizons*, as if it were a jeweller's shop, shewing the goods in different square caskets.

Chap. CLXXII.—*Laughing and Weeping.*

Between the expression of laughter and that of weeping there is no difference in the motion of the features, either in the eyes, mouth, or cheeks; only in the ruffling of the brows, which is added when weeping, but more elevated and extended in laughing. One may represent the figure weeping as tearing his clothes, or some other expression, as various as the cause of his feeling may be; because some weep for anger, some through fear, others for tenderness and joy, or for suspicion; some for real pain and torment; whilst others weep through compassion, or regret at the loss of some friend and near relation. These different feelings will be expressed by some with marks of despair, by others with moderation; some only shed tears, others cry aloud, while an-

* See chap. cxxiii.

other has his face turned towards Heaven, with
his hand depressed, and his fingers twisted. Some
again will be full of apprehension, with their
shoulders raised up to their ears, and so on, according to the above causes.

Those who weep, raise the brows, and bring
them close together above the nose, forming
many wrinkles on the forehead, and the corners
of the mouth are turned downwards. Those who
laugh have them turned upwards, and the brows
open and extended.

Chap. CLXXIII.—*Of Anger.*

If you represent a man in a violent fit of anger,
make him seize another by the hair, holding his
head writhed down against the ground, with his
knee fixed upon the ribs of his antagonist; his
right arm up, and his fist ready to strike; his
hair standing on end, his eyebrows low and
straight; his teeth close, and seen at the corner
of the mouth; his neck swelled, and his body
covered in the abdomen with creases, occasioned
by his bending over his enemy, and the excess of
his passion.

Chap. CLXXIV.—*Despair.*

The last act of despondency is, when a man is
in the act of putting a period to his own existence. He should be represented with a knife in
one hand, with which he has already inflicted the

wound, and tearing it open with the other. His garments and hair should be already torn. He will be standing with his feet asunder, his knees a little bent, and his body leaning forward, as if ready to fall to the ground.

LIGHT AND SHADOW.

Chap. CLXXV.—*The Course of Study to be pursued.*

THE student who is desirous of making great proficiency in the art of imitating the works of Nature, should not only learn the shape of figures or other objects, and be able to delineate them with truth and precision, but he must also accompany them with their proper lights and shadows, according to the situation in which those objects appear.

Chap. CLXXVI.—*Which of the two is the most useful Knowledge, the Outlines of Figures, or that of Light and Shadow.*

The knowledge of the outline is of most consequence, and yet may be acquired to great certainty by dint of study; as the outlines of the different parts of the human figure, particularly those which do not bend, are invariably the same. But the knowledge of the situation, quality, and quantity of shadows, being infinite, requires the most extensive study.

CHAP. CLXXVII.—*Which is the most important, the Shadows or Outlines in Painting.*

It requires much more observation and study to arrive at perfection in the shadowing of a picture, than in merely drawing the lines of it. The proof of this is, that the lines may be traced upon a veil or a flat glass placed between the eye and the object to be imitated. But that cannot be of any use in shadowing, on account of the infinite gradation of shades, and the blending of them, which does not allow of any precise termination; and most frequently they are confused, as will be demonstrated in another place.*

CHAP. CLXXVIII. — *What is a Painter's first Aim and Object.*

The first object of a painter is to make a simple flat surface appear like a relievo, and some of its parts detached from the ground; he who excels all others in that part of the art, deserves the greatest praise. This perfection of the art depends on the correct distribution of lights and shades, called *Chiaro-scuro*. If the painter then avoids shadows, he may be said to avoid the glory of the art, and to render his work despicable to real connoisseurs, for the sake of acquiring the esteem of vulgar and ignorant admirers of fine colours, who never have any knowledge of relievo.

* See chap. cclxiv.

F

CHAP. CLXXIX.—*The Difference of Superficies, in regard to Painting.*

Solid bodies are of two sorts: the one has the surface curvilinear, oval, or spherical; the other has several surfaces, or sides producing angles, either regular or irregular. Spherical, or oval bodies, will always appear detached from their ground, though they are exactly of the same colour. Bodies also of different sides and angles will always detach, because they are always disposed so as to produce shades on some of their sides, which cannot happen to a plain superficies.*

CHAP. CLXXX.—*How a Painter may become universal.*

The painter who wishes to be universal, and please a variety of judges, must unite in the same composition, objects susceptible of great force in the shadows, and great sweetness in the management of them; accounting, however, in every instance, for such boldness and softenings.

CHAP. CLXXXI.—*Accuracy ought to be learnt before Dispatch in the Execution.*

If you wish to make good and useful studies, use great deliberation in your drawings, observe

* See chapter cclxvii.

well among the lights, which, and how many, hold
the first rank in point of brightness; and so
among the shadows, which are darker than others,
and in what manner they blend together; compare the quality and quantity of one with the
other, and observe to what part they are directed.
Be careful also in your outlines, or divisions of
the members.   Remark well what quantity of parts
are to be on one side, and what on the other; and
where they are more or less apparent, or broad,
or slender.   Lastly, take care that the shadows
and lights be united, or lost in each other; without any hard strokes or lines; as smoke loses
itself in the air, so are your lights and shadows to
pass from the one to the other, without any apparent separation.

When you have acquired the habit, and formed
your hand to accuraey, quickness of execution
will come of itself.*

CHAP. CLXXXII.—*How the Painter is to place
himself in regard to the Light, and his Model.*

Let A B be the window, M the centre of it, C
the model.   The best situation for the painter
will be a little sideways, between the window and
his model, as D, so that he may see his object
partly in the light and partly in the shadow.

* Sir Joshua Reynolds frequently inculcated these precepts in
his lectures, and indeed they cannot be too often enforced.

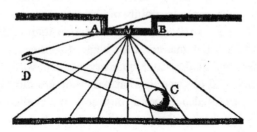

CHAP. CLXXXIII.—*Of the best Light.*

The light from on high, and not too powerful, will be found the best calculated to shew the parts to advantage.

CHAP. CLXXXIV.—*Of Drawing by Candle-light.*

To this artificial light apply a paper blind, and you will see the shadows undetermined and soft.

CHAP. CLXXXV.—*Of those Painters who draw at Home from one Light, and afterwards adapt their studies to another Situation in the Country, and a different Light.*

It is a great error in some painters who draw a figure from nature at home, by any particular light, and afterwards make use of that drawing in a picture representing an open country, which receives the general light of the sky, where the surrounding air gives light on all sides. This painter would put dark shadows, where Nature would either produce none, or, if any, so very faint as to be almost imperceptible; and he would throw reflected lights where it is impossible there should be any.

CHAP. CLXXXVI.—*How high the Light should be in drawing from Nature.*

To paint well from Nature, your window should be to the North, that the lights may not vary. If it be to the South, you must have paper blinds, that the sun, in going round, may not alter the shadows. The situation of the light should be such as to produce upon the ground a shadow from your model as long as that is high.

CHAP. CLXXXVII.—*What Light the Painter must make Use of to give most Relief to his Figures.*

The figures which receive a particular light show more relief than those which receive an universal one; because the particular light occasions some reflexes, which proceed from the light of one object upon the shadows of another, and help to detach it from the dark ground. But a figure placed in front of a dark and large space, and receiving a particular light, can receive no reflexion from any other objects, and nothing is seen of the figure but what the light strikes on, the rest being blended and lost in the darkness of the back ground. This is to be applied only to the imitation of night subjects with very little light.

CHAP. CLXXXVIII.—*Advice to Painters.*

Be very careful, in painting, to observe, that between the shadows there are other shadows, almost imperceptible, both for darkness and shape; and this is proved by the third proposition,* which says, that the surfaces of globular or convex bodies have as great a variety of lights and shadows as the bodies that surround them have.

CHAP. CLXXXIX.—*Of Shadows.*

Those shadows which in Nature are undetermined, and the extremities of which can hardly be perceived, are to be copied in your painting in the same manner, never to be precisely finished, but left confused and blended. This apparent neglect will show great judgment, and be the ingenious result of your observation of Nature.

CHAP. CXC.—*Of the Kind of Light proper for drawing from Relievos, or from Nature.*

Lights separated from the shadows with too much precision, have a very bad effect. In order,

---

* Probably this would have formed a part of his intended Treatise on Light and Shadow, but no such proposition occurs in the present work.

therefore, to avoid this inconvenience, if the object be in the open country, you need not let your figures be illumined by the sun; but may suppose some transparent clouds interposed, so that the sun not being visible, the termination of the shadows will be also imperceptible and soft.

CHAP. CXCI.—*Whether the Light should be admitted in Front or sideways; and which is most pleasing and graceful.*

The light admitted in front of heads situated opposite to side walls that are dark, will cause them to have great relievo, particularly if the light be placed high; and the reason is, that the most prominent parts of those faces are illumined by the general light striking them in front, which light produces very faint shadows on the part where it strikes; but as it turns towards the sides, it begins to participate of the dark shadows of the room, which grow darker in proportion as it sinks into them. Besides, when the light comes from on high, it does not strike on every part of the face alike, but one part produces great shadows upon another; as the eyebrows, which deprive the whole sockets of the eyes of light. The nose keeps it off from great part of the mouth, and the chin from the neck, and such other parts. This, by concentrating the light upon the most projecting parts, produces a very great relief.

CHAP. CXCII.—*Of the Difference of Lights according to the Situation.*

A small light will cast large and determined shadows upon the surrounding bodies. A large light, on the contrary, will cast small shadows on them, and they will be much confused in their termination. When a small but strong light is surrounded by a broad but weaker light, the latter will appear like a demi-tint to the other, as the sky round the sun. And the bodies which receive the light from the one, will serve as demi-tints to those which receive the light from the other.

CHAP. CXCIII.—*How to distribute the Light on Figures.*

The lights are to be distributed according to the natural situation you mean your figures should occupy. If you suppose them in sunshine, the shades must be dark, the lights broad and extended, and the shadows of all the surrounding objects distinctly marked upon the ground. If seen in a gloomy day, there will be very little difference between the lights and shades, and no shadows at the feet. If the figures be represented within doors, the lights and shadows will again be distinctly divided, and produce shadows on the ground. But if you suppose a paper blind at the window, and the walls painted white, the effect will be the same as in a gloomy day, when the lights and shadows have little difference. If the figures are enlightened by the fire, the lights must be red and powerful, the shadows dark, and the shadows upon the ground and upon the walls must be precise; observing that they spread wider as they go off from the body. If the figures be enlightened, partly by the sky and partly by the fire, that side which receives the light from the sky will be the brightest, and on the other side it will be reddish, somewhat of the colour of the fire. Above all, contrive that your figures receive a broad light, and that from above; particularly in portraits, because the people we see in the street receive all the light from above; and it is curious to observe, that there is not a face ever so well known amongst your acquaintance, but would be recognised with difficulty, if it were enlightened from beneath.

CHAP. CXCIV.—*Of the Beauty of Faces.*

You must not mark any muscles with hardness of line, but let the soft light glide upon them, and terminate imperceptibly in delightful shadows: from this will arise grace and beauty to the face.

CHAP. CXCV.—*How, in drawing a Face, to give it Grace, by the Management of Light and Shade.*

A face placed in the dark part of a room, ac-

F 5

quires great additional grace by means of light and shadow. The shadowed part of the face blends with the darkness of the ground, and the light part receives an increase of brightness from the open air, the shadows on this side becoming almost insensible; and from this augmentation of light and shadow, the face has much relief, and acquires great beauty.

Chap. CXCVI.—*How to give Grace and Relief to Faces.*

In streets running towards the west, when the sun is in the meridian, and the walls on each side so high that they cast no reflexions on that side of the bodies which is in shade, and the sky is not too bright, we find the most advantageous situation for giving relief and grace to figures, particularly to faces; because both sides of the face will participate of the shadows of the walls. The sides of the nose and the face towards the west, will be light, and the man whom we supposed placed at the entrance, and in the middle of the street, will see all the parts of that face, which are before him, perfectly illumined, while both sides of it, towards the walls, will be in shadow. What gives additional grace is, that these shades do not appear cutting, hard, or dry, but softly blended and lost in each other. The reason of it is, that the light which is spread all over in the air, strikes also the pavement of the street, and reflecting upon the shady part of the face, it tinges that slightly with the same hue : while the great light which comes from above being confined by the tops of houses, strikes on the face with different points, almost to the very beginning of the shadows under the projecting parts of the face. It diminishes by degrees the strength of them, increasing the light till it comes upon the chin, where it terminates, and loses itself, blending softly into the shades on all sides. For instance, if such light were A E, the line F E would give light even to the bottom of the nose. The line C F will give light only to the under lip; but the line A H would extend the shadow to all the under parts of the face, and under the chin.

In this situation the nose receives a very strong light from all the points A B C D E.

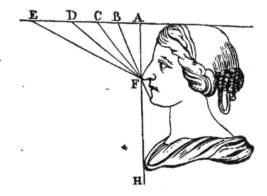

Chap. CXCVII.—*Of the Termination of Bodies upon each other.*

When a body, of a cylindrical or convex surface, terminates upon another body of the same colour, it will appear darker on the edge, than the body upon which it terminates.   And any flat body, adjacent to a white surface, will appear very dark; but upon a dark ground it will appear lighter than any other part, though the lights be equal.

Chap. CXCVIII.—*Of the Back-grounds of painted Objects.*

The ground which surrounds the figures in any painting, ought to be darker than the light part of those figures, and lighter than the shadowed part.

Chap. CXCIX.—*How to detach and bring forward Figures out of their Back-ground.*

If your figure be dark, place it on a light ground; if it be light, upon a dark ground; and if it be partly light and partly dark, as is generally the case, contrive that the dark part of the figure be upon the light part of the ground, and the light side of it against the dark.*

Chap. CC.—*Of proper Back-grounds.*

It is of the greatest importance to consider well

* See chapters cc. and ccxix.

the nature of back-grounds, upon which any opake body is to be placed. In order to detach it properly, you should place the light part of such opake body against the dark part of the back-ground, and the dark parts on a light ground;* as in the cut.†

CHAP. CCI.—*Of the general Light diffused over Figures.*

In compositions of many figures and animals, observe, that the parts of these different objects ought to be darker in proportion as they are lower,

* See chap. ccix.

† This cannot be taken as an absolute rule; it must be left in a great measure to the judgment of the painter. For much graceful softness and grandeur is acquired, sometimes, by blending the lights of the figures with the light part of the ground; and so of the shadows; as Leonardo himself has observed in chapters cxciv. cxcv. and Sir Joshua Reynolds has often put in practice with success.

and as they are nearer the middle of the groups,
though they are all of an uniform colour. This is
necessary, because a smaller proportion of the sky
(from which all bodies are illuminated) can give
light to the lower spaces between these different
figures, than to the upper parts of the spaces. It
is proved thus: A B C D is that portion of the
sky which gives light to all the objects beneath;
M and N are the bodies which occupy the space
S T R H, in which it is evidently perceived, that
the point F, receiving the light only from the
portion of the sky C D, has a smaller quantity of
it than the point E which receives it from the
whole space A B (a larger portion than C D);
therefore it will be lighter in E than in F.

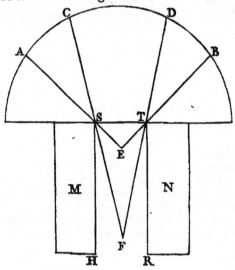

CHAP. CCII.—*Of those Parts in Shadows which*
appear the darkest at a Distance.

THE neck, or any other part which is raised
straight upwards, and has a projection over it,
will be darker than the perpendicular front of
that projection; and this projecting part will be
lighter, in proportion as it presents a larger surface to the light.

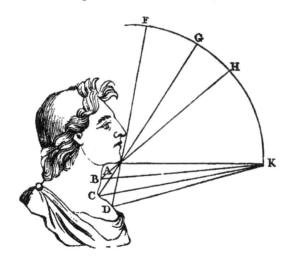

For instance, the recess A receives no light from
any part of the sky G K, but B begins to receive
the light from the part of the sky H K, and C
from G K; and the point D receives the whole of
F K. Therefore the chest will be as light as the

forehead, nose, and chin. But what I have particularly to recommend, in regard to faces, is, that you observe well those different qualities of shades which are lost at different distances (while there remain only the first and principal spots or strokes of shades, such as those of the sockets of the eyes, and other similar recesses, which are always dark), and at last the whole face becomes obscured; because the greatest lights (being small in proportion to the demi-tints) are lost. The quality, therefore, and quantity of the principal lights and shades are by means of great distance blended together into a general half-tint; and this is the reason why trees and other objects are found to be in appearance darker at some distance than they are in reality, when nearer to the eye. But then the air, which interposes between the objects and the eye, will render them light again by tinging them with azure, rather in the shades than in the lights; for the lights will preserve the truth of the different colours much longer.

CHAP. CCIII.—*Of the Eye viewing the Folds of Draperies surrounding a Figure.*

The shadows between the folds of a drapery surrounding the parts of the human body will be darker as the deep hollows where the shadows are generated are more directly opposite the eye.

This is to be observed only when the eye is placed between the light and the shady part of the figure.

CHAP. CCIV.—*Of the Relief of Figures remote from the Eye.*

Any opake body appears less relieved in proportion as it is farther distant from the eye; because the air, interposed between the eye and such body, being lighter than the shadow of it, it tarnishes and weakens that shadow, lessens its power, and consequently lessens also its relief.

CHAP. CCV.—*Of Outlines of Objects on the Side towards the Light.*

The extremities of any object on the side which receives the light, will appear darker if upon a lighter ground, and lighter if seen upon a darker ground. But if such body be flat, and seen upon a ground equal in point of light with itself, and of the same colour, such boundaries, or outlines, will be entirely lost to the sight.*

CHAP. CCVI.—*How to make Objects detach from their Ground, that is to say, from the Surface on which they are painted.*

Objects contrasted with a light ground will appear much more detached than those which are

* See chap. cclxv.

placed against a dark one. The reason is, that if
you wish to give relief to your figures, you will
make those parts which are the farthest from the
light, participate the least of it; therefore they
will remain the darkest, and every distinction of
outline would be lost in the general mass of shadows. But to give it grace, roundness, and effect,
those dark shades are always attended by reflexes, or else they would either cut too hard upon
the ground, or stick to it, by the similarity of
shade, and relieve the less as the ground is darker; for at some distance nothing would be seen
but the light parts, therefore your figures would
appear mutilated of all that remains lost in the
back-ground.

CONTRASTE AND EFFECT.

Chap. CCVII.—*A Precept.*

Figures will have more grace, placed in the
open and general light, than in any particular or
small one; because the powerful and extended
light will surround and embrace the objects: and
works done in that kind of light appear pleasant

and graceful when placed at a distance*, while those which are drawn in a narrow light will receive great force of shadow, but will never appear at a great distance, but as painted objects.

CHAP. CCVIII.—*Of the Interposition of transparent Bodies between the Eye and the Object.*

The greater the transparent interposition is between the eye and the object, the more the colour of that object will participate of, or be changed into that of the transparent medium †.

When an opake body is situated between the eye and the luminary, so that the central line of the one passes also through the centre of the other, that object will be entirely deprived of light.

CHAP. CCIX.—*Of proper Back-grounds for Figures.*

As we find by experience, that all bodies are surrounded by lights and shadows, I would have the painter to accommodate that part which is enlightened, so as to terminate upon something dark; and to manage the dark parts so that they may terminate on a light ground. This will be of

---

* See chap. cxcvi.

† He means here to say, that in proportion as the body interposed between the eye and the object is more or less transparent, the greater or less quantity of the colour of the body interposed will be communicated to the object.

great assistance in detaching and bringing out his
figures.*

Chap. CCX.—*Of Back-grounds.*

To give a great effect to figures, you must oppose to a light one a dark ground, and to a dark
figure a light ground, contrasting white with
black, and black with white. In general, all con-
traries give a particular force and brilliancy of
effect by their opposition.†

REFLEXES.

Chap. CCXI.—*Of Objects placed on a light Ground, and why such a Practice is useful in Painting.*

When a darkish body terminates upon a light
ground, it will appear detached from that ground;
because all opake bodies of a curved surface are
not only dark on that side which receives no light,
and consequently very different from the ground;
but even that side of the curved surface which is
enlightened, will not carry its principal light to

* See the note to chap. cc.
† See the preceding chapter, and chap. co.

flexion has behind it a ground lighter than itself, it will appear dark, in comparison to the brightness which is close to it, and therefore it will be hardly perceptible.*

HAP. CCXVI.—*Of the reflected Lights which surround the Shadows.*

The reflected lights which strike upon the midst shadows, will brighten up or lessen their obscurity in proportion to the strength of those lights, and their proximity to those shadows. Many painters neglect this observation, while others attend to and deduce their practice from it. This difference of opinion and practice divides the sentiments of artists, so that they blame each other for not thinking and acting as they themselves do. The best way is to steer a middle course, and not to admit of any reflected light, but when the cause of it is evident to every eye; and *vice versa*, if you introduce none at all, let it appear evident that there was no reasonable cause for it. In doing so, you will neither be totally blamed nor praised by the variety of opinion, which, if not proceeding from entire ignorance, will ensure to you the approbation of both parties.

CHAP. CCXVII.—*Where Reflexes are to be most apparent.*

Of all reflected lights, that is to be the most ap-

* See chap. ccxvii. and ccxix.

parent, bold, and precise, which detaches from the
darkest ground; and, on the contrary, that which
is upon a lighter ground will be less apparent.
And this proceeds from the contraste of shades,
by which the faintest makes the dark ones appear
still darker; so in contrasted lights, the brightest
cause the others to appear less bright than they
really are.*

CHAP. CCXVIII.—*What Part of a Reflex is to be the lightest.*

That part will be the brightest which receives
the reflected light between angles the most nearly
equal. For example, let N be the luminary, and
A B the illuminated part of the object, reflecting
the light over all the shady part of the concavity
opposite to it. The light which reflects upon F
will be placed between equal angles. But E at
the base will not be reflected by equal angles, as it
is evident that the angle E A B is more obtuse
than the angle E B A. The angle A F B, however,
though it is between angles of less quality than the
angle E, and has a common base B A, is between
angles more nearly equal than E, therefore it will
be lighter in F than in E; and it will also be
brighter, because it is nearer to the part which

* See chap. ccxv. and ccxix.

gives them light, According to the 6th rule,* which says, that part of the body is to be the lightest, which is nearest to the luminary.

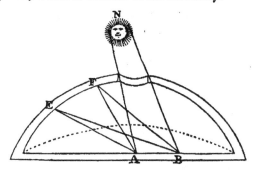

CHAP. CCXIX.—*Of the Termination of Reflexes on their Grounds.*

The termination of a reflected light on a ground lighter than that reflex, will not be perceivable; but if such a reflex terminates upon a ground darker than itself, it will be plainly seen; and the more so in proportion as that ground is darker, and *vice versa.*†

CHAP. CCXX.—*Of double and treble Reflexions of Light.*

¬Double reflexes are stronger than single ones,

* This was intended to constitute a part of some book of Perspective, which we have not; but the rule here referred to will be found in chap cccx. of the present work.

† See chap. ccxv. and ccxvii.

G

and the shadows which interpose between the common light and these reflexes are very faint. For instance, let A be the luminous body, A N, A S, are the direct rays, and S N the parts which receive the light from them. O and E are the places enlightened by the reflexion of that light in those parts. A N E is a single reflex, but A N O, A S O is the double reflex. The single reflex is that which proceeds from a single light, but the double reflexion is produced by two different lights. The single one E is produced by the light striking on B D, while the double one O proceeds from the enlightened bodies B D and D R co-operating together; and the shadows which are between N O and S O will be very faint.

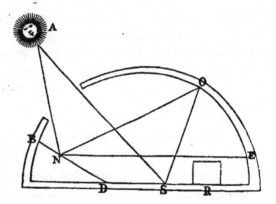

CHAP. CCXXI.—*Reflexes in the Water, and particularly those of the Air.*

The only portion of air that will be seen reflected in the water, will be that which is reflected by the surface of the water to the eye between equal angles; that is to say, the angle of incidence must be equal to the angle of reflexion.

COLOURS AND COLOURING.

COLOURS.

CHAP. CCXXII.—*What Surface is best calculated to receive most Colours.*

WHITE is more capable of receiving all sorts of colours, than the surface of any body whatever, that is not transparent. To prove it, we shall say, that any void space is capable of receiving what another space, not void, cannot receive. In the same manner, a white surface, like a void space, being destitute of any colour, will be fittest to receive such as are conveyed to it from any other enlightened body, and will participate more of the colour than black can do; which latter, like a broken vessel, is not able to contain any thing.

CHAP. CCXXIII.—*What Surface will shew most perfectly its true Colour.*

That opake body will show its colour more perfect and beautiful, which has near it another body of the same colour.

CHAP. CCXXIV.—*On what Surfaces the true Colour is least apparent.*

Polished and glossy surfaces show least of their genuine colour. This is exemplified in the grass of the fields, and the leaves of trees, which, being smooth and glossy, will reflect the colour of the sun, and the air, where they strike, so that the parts which receive the light do not show their natural colour.

CHAP. CCXXV.—*What Surfaces show most of their true and genuine Colour.*

Those objects that are the least smooth and polished shew their natural colours best; as we see in cloth, and in the leaves of such grass or trees as are of a woolly nature; which, having no lustre, are exhibited to the eye in their true natural colour; unless that colour happen to be confused by that of another body casting on them reflexions of an opposite colour, such as the redness of the setting sun, when all the clouds are tinged with its colour.

CHAP. CCXXVI.—*Of the Mixture of Colours.*

Although the mixture of colours may be extended to an infinite variety, almost impossible to be described, I will not omit touching slightly upon it, setting down at first a certain number of simple

colours to serve as a foundation, and with each of
these mixing one of the others; one with one, then
two with two, and three with three, proceeding in
this manner to the full mixture of all the colours
together: then I would begin again, mixing two
of these colours with·two others, and three with
three, four with four, and so on to the end. To
these two colours we shall put three; to these
three add three more, and then six, increasing
always in the same proportion.

I call those simple colours, which are not composed, and cannot be made or supplied by any
mixture of other colours. Black and White are
not reckoned among colours; the one is the representative of darkness, the other of light: that is,
one is a simple privation of light, the other is light
itself. Yet I will not omit mentioning them, because there is nothing in painting more useful and
necessary; since painting is but an effect produced
by lights and shadows, viz. *chiara-scuro*. After
Black and White come Blue and Yellow, then
Green, and Tawny or Umber, and then Purple
and Red. These eight colours are all that Nature
produces. With these I begin my mixtures, first
Black and White, Black and Yellow, Black and
Red; then Yellow and Red: but I shall treat
more at length of these mixtures in a separate
work,* which will be of great utility, nay very ne-

* No such work was ever published, nor, for any thing that
appears, ever written.

cessary. I shall place this subject between theory and practice.

CHAP. CCXXVII.—*Of the Colours produced by the Mixture of other Colours, called secondary Colours.*

The first of all simple colours is White, though philosophers will not acknowledge either White or Black to be colours; because the first is the cause, or the receiver of colours, the other totally deprived of them. But as painters cannot do without either, we shall place them among the others; and according to this order of things, White will be the first, Yellow the second, Green the third, Blue the fourth, Red the fifth, and Black the sixth. We shall set down White for the representative of light, without which no colour can be seen; Yellow for the earth; Green for water; Blue for air; Red for fire; and Black for total darkness.

If you wish to see by a short process the variety of all the mixed, or composed colours, take some coloured glasses, and, through them, look at all the country round: you will find that the colour of each object will be altered and mixed with the colour of the glass through which it is seen; observe which colour is made better, and which is hurt by the mixture. If the glass be yellow, the colour of the objects may either be improved, or greatly impaired by it. Black and White will be most altered, while Green and Yellow will be meliorated. In the same manner you may go through all the mixtures of colours, which are infinite. Select those which are new and agreeable to the sight; and following the same method you may go on with two glasses, or three, till you have found what will best answer your purpose.

CHAP. CCXXVIII.—*Of Verdegris.*

This green, which is made of copper, though it be mixed with oil, will lose its beauty, if it be not varnished immediately. It not only fades, but, if washed with a sponge and pure water only, it will detach from the ground upon which it is painted, particularly in damp weather; because verdegris is produced by the strength of salts, which easily dissolve in rainy weather, but still more if washed with a wet sponge.

CHAP. CCXXIX.—*How to increase the Beauty of Verdegris.*

If you mix with the Verdegris some Caballine Aloe, it will add to it a great degree of beauty. It would acquire still more from Saffron, if it did not fade. The quality and goodness of this Aloe will be proved by dissolving it in warm Brandy. Supposing the Verdigris has already been used, and the part finished, you may then glaze it thinly with this dissolved Aloe, and it will produce a very fine colour. This Aloe may be ground also in oil by itself, or with the Verdegris, or any other co-lour, at pleasure.

CHAP. CCXXX.—*How to paint a Picture that will last almost for ever.*

· After you have made a drawing of your in-tended picture, prepare a good and thick priming with pitch and brickdust well pounded; after which give it a second coat of white lead and Naples yellow; then, having traced your drawing upon it, and painted your picture, varnish it with clear and thick old oil, and stick it to a flat glass, or crystal, with a clear varnish. Another method, which may be better, is, instead of the priming of pitch and brickdust, take a flat tile well vitrified, then apply the coat of white and Naples yellow, and all the rest as before. But before the glass is applied to it, the painting must be perfectly dried in a stove, and varnished with nut oil and amber, or else with purified nut oil alone, thickened in the sun.*

* The French translation of 1716 has a note on this chapter, saying, that the invention of enamel painting found out since the time of Leonardo da Vinci, would better answer to the title of this chapter, and also be a better method of painting. I must beg leave, however, to dissent from this opinion, as the two kinds of painting are so different that they cannot be compared. Leo-nardo treats of oil painting, but the other is vitrification. Leo-nardo is known to have spent a great deal of time in experiments, of which this is a specimen, and it may appear ridiculous to the

CHAP. CCXXXI.—*The Mode of painting on Canvass, or Linen Cloth*.*

STRETCH your canvass upon a frame, then give it a coat of weak size, let it dry, and draw your outlines upon it. Paint the flesh colours first; and while it is still fresh or moist, paint also the shadows, well softened and blended together. The flesh colour may be made with white, lake, and Naples yellow. The shades with black, umber, and a little lake; you may, if you please, use black chalk. After you have softened this first coat, or dead colour, and let it dry, you may retouch over it with lake and other colours, and gum water that has been a long while made and kept liquid, because in that state it becomes better, and does not leave any gloss. Again, to make the shades darker, take the lake and gum as above, and ink*; and with this you may shade or glaze many colours, because it is transparent; such as azure, lake, and several others. As for

practitioners of more modern date, as he does not enter more fully into a minute description of the materials, or the mode of employing them. The principle laid down in the text appears to me to be simply this: to make the oil entirely evaporate from the colours by the action of fire, and afterwards to prevent the action of the air by the means of a glass which in itself is an excellent principle, but not applicable, any more than enamel painting, to large works.

* It is evident that distemper or size painting is here meant.
† Indian ink.

the lights, you may retouch or glaze them slightly
with gum water and pure lake, particularly vermi
lion.

CHAP. CCXXXII.—*Of lively and beautiful*
Colours.

For those colours which you mean should appear beautiful, prepare a ground of pure white.
This is meant only for transparent colours : as for
those that have a body, and are opake, it matters
not what ground they have, and a white one is of
no use. This is exemplified by painted glasses;
when placed between the eye and clear air, they
exhibit most excellent and beautiful colours, which
is not the case, when they have thick air, or some
opake body behind them.

CHAP. CCXXXIII.—*Of transparent Colours.*

WHEN a transparent colour is laid upon another of a different nature, it produces a mixed
colour, different from either of the simple ones
which compose it. This is observed in the smoke
coming out of a chimney, which, when passing
before the black soot, appears blueish, but as it
ascends against the blue of the sky, it changes its
appearance into a reddish brown. So the colour
lake laid on blue will turn it to a violet colour;
yellow upon blue turns to green; saffron upon
white becomes yellow; white scumbled upon a

dark ground appears blue, and is more or less beautiful, as the white and the ground are more or less pure.

CHAP. CCXXXIV.—*In what Part a Colour will appear in its greatest Beauty.*

We are to consider here in what part any colour will shew itself in its most perfect purity; whether in the strongest light or deepest shadow, in the demi-tint, or in the reflex. It would be necessary to determine first, of what colour we mean to treat, because different colours differ materially in that respect. Black is most beautiful in the shades; white in the strongest light; blue and green in the half-tint; yellow and red in the principal light; gold in the reflexes; and lake in the half-tint.

CHAP. CCXXXV.—*How any Colour without a Gloss, is more beautiful in the Lights than in the Shades.*

All objects which have no gloss, shew their colours better in the light than in the shadow, because the light vivifies and gives a true knowledge of the nature of the colour, while the shadows lower, and destroy its beauty, preventing the discovery of its nature. If, on the contrary, black be more beautiful in the shadows, it is because black is not a colour.

Chap. CCXXXVI.—*Of the Appearance of Colours.*

The lighter a colour is in its nature, the more so it will appear when removed to some distance; but with dark colours it is quite the reverse.

Chap. CCXXXVII.—*What Part of a Colour is to be the most beautiful.*

If A be the light, and B the object receiving it in a direct line, E cannot receive that light, but only the reflexion from B, which we shall suppose to be red. In that case, the light it produces being red, it will tinge with red the object E; and if E happen to be also red before, you will see that colour increase in beauty, and appear redder than B; but if E were yellow, you will see a new colour, participating of the red and the yellow.

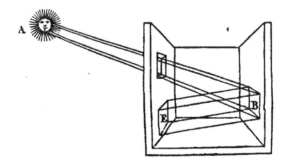

CHAP. CCXXXVIII.—*That the beauty of a Colour is to be found in the Lights.*

As the quality of colours is discovered to the eye by the light, it is natural to conclude, that where there is most light, there also the true quality of the colour is to be seen; and where there is most shadow the colour will participate of, and be tinged with the colour of that shadow. Remember then to shew the true quality of the colour in the light parts only*.

CHAP. CCXXXIX.—*Of Colours.*

The colour which is between the light and the shadow will not be so beautiful as that which is in the full light. Therefore the chief beauty of colours will be found in the principal lights†.

CHAP. CCXL.—*No Object appears in its true Colour, unless the Light which strikes upon it be of the same Colour.*

This is very observable in draperies, where the light folds casting a reflexion, and throwing a light on other folds opposite to them, make them appear in their natural colour. The same effect is produced by gold leaves casting their light reciprocally on each other. The effect is quite con-

* This rule is not without exception : see chap. ccxxxiv.
† See chap. ccxxxviii.

trary if the light be received from an object of a
different colour*.

CHAP. CCXLI.—*Of the Colour of Shadows.*

The colour of the shadows of an object can
never be pure if the body which is opposed to
these shadows be not of the same colour as that
on which they are produced. For instance, if in
a room, the walls of which are green, I place a
figure clothed in blue, and receiving the light from
another blue object, the light part of that figure
will be of a beautiful blue, but the shadows of it
will become dingy, and not like a true shade of
that beautiful blue, because it will be corrupted
by the reflexions from the green wall; and it
would be still worse if the walls were of a darkish
brown.

CHAP. CCXLII.—*Of Colours.*

COLOURS placed in shadow will preserve more
or less of their original beauty, as they are more
or less immersed in the shade. But colours situated in a light space will shew their natural
beauty in proportion to the brightness of that
light. Some say, that there is as great variety in
the colours of shadows, as in the colours of objects shaded by them. It may be answered, that

---

* See chap. ccxxxvii.

colours placed in shadow will shew less variety amongst themselves as the shadows are darker. We shall soon convince ourselves of this truth, if, from a large square, we look through the open door of a church, where pictures, though enriched with a variety of colours, appear all clothed in darkness.

CHAP. CCXLIII.—*Whether it be possible for all Colours to appear alike by means of the same Shadow.*

It is very possible that all the different colours may be changed into that of a general shadow; as is manifest in the darkness of a cloudy night, in which neither the shape nor colour of bodies is distinguished. Total darkness being nothing but a privation of the primitive and reflected lights, by which the form and colour of bodies are seen; it is evident, that the cause being removed the effect ceases, and the objects are entirely lost to the sight.

CHAP. CCXLIV.—*Why White is not reckoned among the Colours.*

White is not a colour, but has the power of receiving all the other colours. When it is placed in a high situation in the country, all its shades are azure; according to the fourth proposition*, which says, that the surface of any opake body participates of the colour of any other body sending the light to it. Therefore white being deprived of the light of the sun by the interposition of any other body, will remain white; if exposed to the sun on one side, and to the open air on the other, it will participate both of the colour of the sun and of the air. That side which is not opposed to the sun, will be shaded of the colour of the air. And if this white were not surrounded by green fields all the way to the horizon, nor could receive any light from that horizon, without doubt it would appear of one simple and uniform colour, viz. that of the air.

Chap. CCXLV.—*Of Colours.*

The light of the fire tinges every thing of a reddish yellow; but this will hardly appear evident, if we do not make the comparison with the daylight. Towards the close of the evening this is easily done; but more certainly after the morning twilight; and the difference will be clearly distinguished in a dark room, when a little glimpse of daylight strikes upon any part of the room, and

* See chapters ccxlvii. cclxxiv. in the present work. Probably they were intended to form a part of a distinct treatise, and to have been ranged as propositions in that, but at present they are not so placed.

there still remains a candle burning. Without such a trial the difference is hardly perceivable, particularly in those colours which have most similarity; such as white and yellow, light green and light blue; because the light which strikes the blue, being yellow, will naturally turn it green; as we have said in another place,* that a mixture of blue and yellow produces green. And if to a green colour you add some yellow, it will make it of a more beautiful green.

CHAP. CCXLVI.—*Of the Colouring of remote Objects.*

The painter who is to represent objects at some distance from the eye, ought merely to convey the idea of general undetermined masses, making choice, for that purpose, of cloudy weather, or towards the evening, and avoiding, as was said before, to mark the lights and shadows too strong on the extremities; because they would in that case appear like spots of difficult execution, and without grace. He ought to remember, that the shadows are never to be of such a quality, as to obliterate the proper colour, in which they originated; if the situation of the coloured body be not in total darkness. He ought to mark no outline, not to make the hair stringy, and not to touch with pure white, any but those things which in

* See chap. ccxlviii.

themselves are white; in short, the lightest touch upon any particular object ought to denote the beauty of its proper and natural colour.

CHAP. CCXLVII.—*The Surface of all opake Bodies participates of the Colour of the surrounding Objects.*

The painter ought to know, that if any white object is placed between two walls, one of which is also white, and the other black, there will be found between the shady side of that object and the light side, a similar proportion to that of the two walls; and if that object be blue, the effect will be the same. Having therefore to paint this object, take some black, similar to that of the wall from which the reflexes come; and to proceed by a certain and scientific method, do as follows. When you paint the wall, take a small spoon to measure exactly the quantity of colour you mean to employ in mixing your tints; for instance, if you have put in the shading of this wall three spoonfuls of pure black, and one of white, you have, without any doubt, a mixture of a certain and precise quality. Now having painted one of the walls white, and the other dark, if you mean to place a blue object between them with shades suitable to that colour, place first on your pallet the light blue, such as you mean it to be, without any mixture of shade, and it will do for the lightest

part of your object. After which take three spoonfuls of black, and one of this light blue, for your
darkest shades. Then observe whether your object
be round or square: if it be square, these two extreme tints of light and shade will be close to each
other, cutting sharply at the angle; but if it be
round, draw lines from the extremities of the walls
to the centre of the object, and put the darkest
shade between equal angles, where the lines intersect upon the superficies of it; then begin to make
them lighter and lighter gradually to the point
N O, lessening the strength of the shadows as
much as that place participates of the light A D,
and mixing that colour with the darkest shade
A B, in the same proportion.

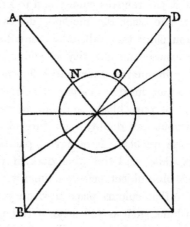

CHAP. CCXLVIII.—*General Remarks on Colours.*

Blue and green are not simple colours in their nature, for blue is composed of light and darkness; such is the azure of the sky, viz. perfect black and perfect white. Green is composed of a simple and a mixed colour, being produced by blue and yellow.

Any object seen in a mirror, will participate of the colour of that body which serves as a mirror; and the mirror in its turn is tinged in part by the colour of the object it represents; they partake more or less of each other as the colour of the object seen is more or less strong than the colour of the mirror. That object will appear of the strongest and most lively colour in the mirror, which has the most affinity to the colour of the mirror itself.

Of coloured bodies, the purest white will be seen at the greatest distance, therefore the darker the colour, the less it will bear distance.

Of different bodies equal in whiteness, and in distance from the eye, that which is surrounded by the greatest darkness will appear the whitest; and on the contrary, that shadow will appear the darkest which has the brightest white round it.

Of different colours, equally perfect, that will appear most excellent, which is seen near its direct contrary. A pale colour against red, a black upon white (though neither the one nor the other are colours); blue near a yellow; green near red; because each colour is more distinctly seen, when opposed to its contrary, than to any other similar to it.

Any thing white seen in a dense air full of vapours, will appear larger than it is in reality.

The air, between the eye and the object seen, will change the colour of that object into its own; so will the azure of the air change the distant mountains into blue masses. Through a red glass every thing appears red; the light round the stars is dimmed by the darkness of the air, which fills the space between the eye and the planets.

The true colour of any object whatever will be seen in those parts which are not occupied by any kind of shade, and have not any gloss (if it be a polished surface).

I say, that white terminating abruptly upon a dark ground, will cause that part where it terminates to appear darker, and the white whiter.

COLOURS IN REGARD TO LIGHT AND SHADOW.

CHAP. CCXLIX.—*Of the Light proper for painting Flesh Colour from Nature.*

YOUR window must be open to the sky, and the walls painted of a reddish colour. The summer-time is the best, when the clouds conceal the sun, or else your walls on the south side of the room must be so high, as that the sun-beams cannot strike on the opposite side, in order that the reflexion of those beams may not destroy the shadows.

CHAP. CCL.—*Of the Painter's Window.*

The window which gives light to a painting-room, ought to be made of oiled paper, without any cross bar, or projecting edge at the opening, or any sharp angle in the inside of the wall, but should be slanting by degrees the whole thickness of it; and the sides be painted black.

CHAP.—CCLI.—*The Shadows of Colours.*

The shadows of any colour whatever must participate of that colour more or less, as it is nearer to, or more remote from, the mass of shadows; and also in proportion to its distance from, or proximity to, the mass of light.

CHAP. CCLII.—*Of the Shadows of White.*

To any white body receiving the light from the sun, or the air, the shadows should be of a blueish cast; because white is no colour, but a receiver of all colours; and as by the fourth proposition * we learn, that the surface of any object participates of the colours of other objects near it, it is evident that a white surface will participate of the colour of the air by which it is surrounded.

CHAP. CCLIII.—*Which of the Colours will produce the darkest Shade.*

That shade will be the darkest which is produced by the whitest surface; this also will have a greater propensity to variety than any other surface; because white is not properly a colour, but a receiver of colours, and its surface will participate strongly of the colour of surrounding objects, but principally of black or any other dark colour, which being the most opposite to its nature, produces the most sensible difference between the shadows and the lights.

* See chap. cclxxiv.

Chap. CCLIV.—*How to manage, when a White terminates upon another White.*

When one white body terminates on another of the same colour, the white of these two bodies will be either alike or not. If they be alike, that object which of the two is nearest to the eye, should be made a little darker than the other, upon the rounding of the outline; but if the object which serves as a ground to the other be not quite so white, the latter will detach of itself, without the help of any darker termination.

Chap. CCLV.—*On the Back-grounds of Figures.*

Of two objects equally light, one will appear less so if seen upon a whiter ground; and, on the contrary, it will appear a great deal lighter if upon a space of a darker shade. So flesh colour will appear pale upon a red ground, and a pale colour will appear redder upon a yellow ground. In short, colours will appear what they are not, according to the ground which surrounds them.

Chap. CCLVI.—*The Mode of composing History.*

Amongst the figures which compose an historical picture, those which are meant to appear the nearest to the eye, must have the greatest force; according to the second proposition* of the third

* Although the author seems to have designed that this, and many other propositions to which he refers, should have formed

H

book, which says, that colour will be seen in the greatest perfection which has less air interposed between it and the eye of the beholder; and for that reason the shadows (by which we express the relievo of bodies) appear darker when near than when at a distance, being then deadened by the air which interposes. This does not happen to those shadows which are near the eye, where they will produce the greatest relievo when they are darkest.

CHAP. CCLVII.—*Remarks concerning Lights and Shadows.*

Observe, that where the shadows end, there be always a kind of half-shadow to blend them with the lights. The shadow derived from any object will mix more with the light at its termination, in proportion as it is more distant from that object. But the colour of the shadow will never be simple; this is proved by the ninth proposition,* which

a part of some regular work, and he has accordingly referred to them whenever he has mentioned them, by their intended nume- rical situation in that work, whatever it might be, it does not appear that he ever carried this design into execution. There are, however, several chapters in the present work, viz. ccxciii. cclxxxix. cclxxxv. coxcv. in which the principle in the text is recognised, and which propably would have been transferred into the projected treatise, if he had ever drawn it up.

* The note on the preceding chapter is in a great measure appli- cable to this, and the proposition mentioned in the text is also to be found in chapter ccxlvii. of the present work.

says, that the superficies of any object participates
of the colours of other bodies, by which it is surrounded, although it were transparent, such as
water, air, and the like : because the air receives
its light from the sun, and darkness is produced
by the privation of it.   But as the air has no colour in itself any more than water, it receives all
the colours that are between the object and the
eye. The vapours mixing with the air in the lower
regions near the earth, render it thick, and apt to
reflect the sun's rays on all sides, while the air
above remains dark; and because light (that is,
white) and darkness (that is, black), mixed together, compose the azure that becomes the colour
of the sky, which is lighter or darker in proportion as the air is more or less mixed with damp
vapours.

CHAP. CCLVIII.—*Why the Shadows of Bodies
upon a white Wall are blueish towards Evening.*

The shadows of bodies produced by the redness
of the setting sun, will always be bluish. This is
accounted for by the eleventh proposition,* which
says, that the superficies of any opake body participates of the colour of the object from which it
receives the light; therefore the white wall being
deprived entirely of colour, is tinged by the colour

* See the note on the chapter next but one preceding. The
proposition in the text occurs in chap. ccxlvii. of the present
work.

of those bodies from which it receives the light, which in this case are the sun and sky. But because the sun is red towards the evening, and the sky is blue, the shadow on the wall not being enlightened by the sun, receives only the reflexion of the sky, and therefore will appear blue; and the rest of the wall, receiving light immediately from the sun, will participate of its red colour.

CHAP. CCLIX.—*Of the Colour of Faces.*

The colour of any object will appear more or less distinct in proportion to the extent of its surface. This proposition is proved, by observing that a face appears dark at a small distance, because, being composed of many small parts, it produces a great number of shadows; and the lights being the smallest part of it, are soonest lost to the sight, leaving only the shadows, which being in a greater quantity, the whole of the face appears dark, and the more so if that face has on the head, or at the back, something whiter.

Chap. CCLX.—*A Precept relating to Painting.*

Where the shadows terminate upon the lights, observe well what parts of them are lighter than the others, and where they are more or less softened and blended; but above all remember, that young people have no sharp shadings: their flesh is transparent, something like what we observe when we put our hand between the sun and eyes; it appears reddish, and of a transparent brightness. If you wish to know what kind of shadow will suit the flesh colour you are painting, place one of your fingers close to your picture, so as to cast a shadow upon it, and according as you wish it either lighter or darker, put it nearer or farther from it, and imitate it.

Chap. CCLXI.—*Of Colours in Shadow.*

It happens very often that the shadows of an opake body do not retain the same colour as the lights. Sometimes they will be greenish, while the lights are reddish, although this opake body be all over of one uniform colour. This happens when the light falls upon the object (we will suppose from the East), and tinges that side with its own colour. In the West we will suppose another opake body of a colour different from the first, but receiving the same light. This last will reflect its colour towards the East, and strike the first with its rays on the opposite side, where they will be stopped, and remain with their full colour and brightness. We often see a white object with red lights, and the shades of a blueish cast; this we observe particularly in mountains covered with snow, at sun-set, when the effulgence of its rays makes the horizon appear all on fire.

CHAP. CCLXII.—*Of the Choice of Lights.*

Whatever object you intend to represent is to be supposed situated in a particular light, and that entirely of your own choosing. If you imagine such objects to be in the country, and the sun be overcast, they will be surrounded by a great quantity of general light. If the sun strikes upon those objects, then the shadows will be very dark, in proportion to the lights, and will be determined and sharp; the primitive as well as the secondary ones. These shadows will vary from the lights in colour, because on that side the object receives a reflected light hue from the azure of the air, which tinges that part; and this is particularly observable in white objects. That side which receives the light from the sun, participates also of the colour of that. This may be particularly observed in the evening, when the sun is setting between the clouds, which it reddens; those clouds being tinged with the colour of the body illuminating them, the red colour of the clouds, with that of the sun, casts a hue on those parts which receive the light from them. On the contrary, those parts which are not turned towards that side of the sky, remain of the colour of the air, so that the former and the latter are of two different colours. This we must not lose sight of, that, knowing the cause of those lights and shades, it be made apparent in the effect, or else the work will be false and absurd. But if a figure be situated within a house, and seen from without, such figure will have its shadows very soft; and if the beholder stands in the line of the light, it will acquire grace, and do credit to the painter, as it will have great relief in the lights, and soft and well-blended shadows, particularly in those parts where the inside of the room appears less obscure, because there the shadows are almost imperceptible: the cause of which we shall explain in its proper place.

COLOURS IN REGARD TO BACK-GROUNDS.

———

CHAP. CCLXIII.—*Of avoiding hard Outlines.*

Do not make the boundaries of your figures with any other colour than that of the back-ground on which they are placed; that is, avoid making dark outlines.

CHAP. CCLXIV.—*Of Outlines.*

The extremities of objects which are at some distance, are not seen so distinctly as if they were nearer. Therefore the painter ought to regulate the strength of his outlines, or extremities, according to the distance.

The boundaries which separate one body from another, are of the nature of mathematical lines, but not of real lines. The end of any colour is only the beginning of another, and it ought not to be called a line, for nothing interposes between them, except the termination of the one against the other, which being nothing in itself, cannot be perceivable; therefore the painter ought not to pronounce it in distant objects.

CHAP. CCLXV.—*Of Back-grounds.*

One of the principal parts of painting is the

nature and quality of back-grounds, upon which
the extremities of any convex or solid body will
always detach and be distinguished in nature,
though the colour of such objects, and that of the
ground, be exactly the same. This happens, because the convex sides of solid bodies do not receive the light in the same manner with the
ground, for such sides or extremities are often
lighter or darker than the ground. But if such
extremities were to be of the same colour as the
ground, and in the same degree of light, they certainly could not be distinguished. Therefore
such a choice in painting ought to be avoided by
all intelligent and judicious painters; since the
intention is to make the object appear as it were
out of the ground. The above case would produce the contrary effect, not only in painting, but
also in objects of real relievo.

CHAP. CCLXVI.—*How to detach Figures from
the Ground.*

All solid bodies will appear to have a greater
relief, and to come more out of the canvass, on a
ground of an undetermined colour, with the greatest variety of lights and shades against the confines of such bodies (as will be demonstrated in
its place), provided a proper diminution of lights
in the white tints, and of darkness in the shades,
be judiciously observed.

CHAP. CCLXVII.—*Of Uniformity and Variety of Colours upon plain Surfaces.*

The back-grounds of any flat surfaces which are uniform in colour and quantity of light, will never appear separated from each other; *vice versâ*, they will appear separated if they are of different colours or lights.

CHAP. CCLXVIII.—*Of Back-grounds suitable both to Shadows and Lights.*

The shadows or lights which surround figures, or any other objects, will help the more to detach them the more they differ from the objects; that is, if a dark colour does not terminate upon another dark colour, but upon a very different one; as white, or partaking of white, but lowered, and approximated to the dark shade.

CHAP. CCLXIX.—*The apparent Variation of Colours, occasioned by the Contraste of the Ground upon which they are placed.*

No colour appears uniform and equal in all its parts, unless it terminate on a ground of the same colour. This is very apparent when a black terminates on a white ground, where the contraste of colour gives more strength and richness to the extremities than to the middle.

CONTRASTE, HARMONY, AND REFLEX-ES, IN REGARD TO COLOURS.

CHAP. CCLXX.—*Gradation in Painting.*

WHAT is fine is not always beautiful and good: I address this to such painters as are so attached to the beauty of colours, that they regret being obliged to give them almost imperceptible shadows, not considering the beautiful relief which figures acquire by a proper gradation and strength of shadows. Such persons may be compared to those speakers who in conversation make use of many fine words without meaning, which altogether scarcely form one good sentence.

CHAP. CCLXXI.—*How to assort Colours in such a Manner as that they may add Beauty to each other.*

If you mean that the proximity of one colour should give beauty to another that terminates near it, observe the rays of the sun in the composition of the rainbow, the colours of which are generated by the falling rain, when each drop in its descent takes every colour of that bow, as is demonstrated in its place*.

* Not in this work.

If you mean to represent great darkness, it must be done by contrasting it with great light; on the contrary, if you want to produce great brightness, you must oppose to it a very dark shade : so a pale yellow will cause red to appear more beautiful than if opposed to a purple colour.

There is another rule, by observing which, though you do not increase the natural beauty of the colours, yet by bringing them together they may give additional grace to each other, as green placed near red, while the effect would be quite the reverse, if placed near blue.

Harmony and grace are also produced by a judicious arrangement of colours, such as blue with pale yellow or white, and the like; as will be noticed in its place.

Chap. CCLXXII.—*Of detaching the Figures.*

Let the colours of which the draperies of your figures are composed, be such as to form a pleasing variety, to distinguish one from the other; and although, for the sake of harmony, they should be of the same nature*, they must not stick toge-

* I do not know a better comment on this passage than Felibien's Examination of Le Brun's Picture of the Tent of Darius. From this (which has been reprinted with an English translation by Colonel Parsons, in 1700, in folio,) it will clearly appear, what the chain of connexion is between every colour there used, and its nearest neighbour, and consequently a rule may be formed from it

ther, but vary in point of light, according to the distance and interposition of the air between them. By the same rule, the outlines are to be more precise, or lost, in proportion to their distance or proximity.

CHAP. CCLXXIII.—*Of the Colour of Reflexes.*

All reflected colours are less brilliant and strong, than those which receive a direct light, in the same proportion as there is between the light of a body and the cause of that light.

CHAP. CCLXXIV.—*What Body will be the most strongly tinged with the Colour of any other Object.*

An opake surface will partake most of the genuine colour of the body nearest to it, because a great quantity of the species of colour will be conveyed to it; whereas such colour would be broken and disturbed if coming from a more distant object.

CHAP. CCLXXV.—*Of Reflexes.*

Reflexes will partake, more or less, both of the colour of the object which produces them, and of the colour of that object on which they are

with more certainty and precision than where the student is left to develope it for himself, from the mere inspection of different examples of colouring.

produced, in proportion as this latter body is of a smoother or more polished surface, than that by which they are produced.

Chap. CCLXXVI.—*Of the Surface of all shadowed Bodies.*

The surface of any opake body placed in shadow, will participate of the colour of any other object which reflects the light upon it. This is very evident; for if such bodies were deprived of light in the space between them and the other bodies, they could not shew either shape or colour. We shall conclude then, that if the opake body be yellow, and that which reflects the light blue, the part reflected will be green, because green is composed of blue and yellow.

Chap. CCLXXVII.—*That no reflected Colour is simple, but is mixed with the nature of the other Colours.*

No colour reflected upon the surface of another body, will tinge that surface with its own colour alone, but will be mixed by the concurrence of other colours also reflected on the same spot. Let us suppose A to be of a yellow colour, which is reflected on the convex C O E, and that the blue colour B be reflected on the same place. I say that a mixture of the blue and yellow colours will tinge the convex surface; and that, if the

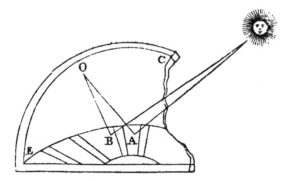

ground be white, it will produce a green reflexion, because it is proved that a mixture of blue and yellow produces a very fine green.

Chap. CCLXXVIII.—*Of the Colour of Lights and Reflexes.*

When two lights strike upon an opake body, they can vary only in two ways; either they are equal in strength, or they are not. If they be equal, they may still vary in two other ways, that is, by the equality or inequality of their brightness; they will be equal, if their distance be the same; and unequal, if it be otherwise. The object placed at an equal distance, between two equal lights, in point both of colour and brightness, may still be enlightened by them in two different ways, either equally on each side, or unequally. It will be equally enlightened by them, when the space which remains round the lights shall be equal in colour, in degree of shade, and in brightness. It will be unequally enlightened by them when the spaces happen to be of different degrees of darkness.

CHAP. CCLXXIX.—*Why reflected Colours seldom partake of the Colour of the Body where they meet.*

It happens very seldom that the reflexes are of the same colour with the body from which they proceed, or with that upon which they meet. To exemplify this, let the convex body D F G E be of a yellow colour, and the body B C, which reflects its colour on it, blue; the part of the convex surface which is struck by that reflected light, will take a green tinge, being B C, acted on by the natural light of the air or the sun.

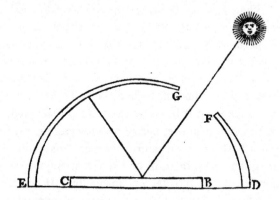

CHAP. CCLXXX.—*The Reflexes of Flesh Colours.*

The lights upon the flesh colours, which are reflected by the light striking upon another flesh-coloured body, are redder and more lively than any other part of the human figure; and that happens according to the third proposition of the second book,* which says, the surface of any opake body participates of the colour of the object which reflects the light in proportion as it is near to or remote from it, and also in proportion to the size of it; because, being large, it prevents the variety of colours in smaller objects round it, from interfering with, and discomposing the principal colour, which is nearer.   Nevertheless it does not prevent its participating more of the colour of a small object near it, than of a large one more remote.   See the sixth proposition† of perspective, which says, that large objects may be situated at such a distance as to appear less than small ones that are near.

---

* See chap. ccxxiii. ccxxxvii. cclxxiv. cclxxxii. of the present work. We have before remarked, that the propositions so frequently referred to by the author, were never reduced into form, though apparently he intended a regular work in which they were to be included.

† No where in this work.

CHAP. CCLXXXI.—*Of the Nature of Comparison.*

Black draperies will make the flesh of the human figure appear whiter than in reality it is ;* and white draperies, on the contrary, will make it appear darker. Yellow will render it higher coloured, while red will make it pale.

CHAP. CCLXXXII.—*Where the Reflexes are seen.*

Of all reflexions of the same shape, size, and strength, that will be more or less strong, which terminates on a ground more or less dark.

The surface of those bodies will partake most of the colour of the object that reflects it, which receive that reflexion by the most nearly equal angles.

Of the colours of objects reflected upon any opposite surface by equal angles, that will be the most distinct which has its reflecting ray the shortest.

Of all colours, reflected under equal angles, and at equal distance upon the opposite body, those will be the strongest, which come reflected by the lightest coloured body.

That object will reflect its own colour most precisely on the opposite object, which has not round

* This is evident in many of Vandyke's portraits, particularly of ladies, many of whom are dressed in black velvet ; and this remark will in some measure account for the delicate fairness which he frequently gives to the female complexion.

it any colour that clashes with its own; and consequently that reflected colour will be most confused which takes its origin from a variety of bodies of different colours.

That colour which is nearest the opposed object, will tinge it the most strongly; and *vice versâ:* let the painter, therefore, in his reflexes on the human body, particularly on the flesh colour, mix some of the colour of the drapery which comes nearest to it; but not pronounce it too distinctly, if there be not good reason for it.

PERSPECTIVE OF COLOURS.

CHAP. CCLXXXIII.—*A Precept of Perspective in regard to Painting.*

WHEN, on account of some particular quality of the air, you can no longer distinguish the difference between the lights and shadows of objects, you may reject the perspective of shadows, and make use only of the linear perspective, and the diminution of colours, to lessen the knowledge of the objects opposed to the eye; and this, that is to say, the loss of the knowledge of the figure of each object, will make the same object appear more remote.

The eye can never arrive at a perfect knowledge of the interval between two objects variously distant, by means of the linear perspective alone, if not assisted by the perspective of colours.

CHAP. CCLXXXIV.—*Of the Perspective of Colours.*

The air will participate less of the azure of the sky, in proportion as it comes nearer to the horizon, as it is proved by the third and ninth proposition,* that pure and subtile bodies (such as compose the air) will be less illuminated by the sun than those of thicker and grosser substance : and as it is certain that the air which is remote from the earth, is thinner than that which is near it, it will follow, that the latter will be more impreg · nated with the rays of the sun, which giving light at the same time to an infinity of atoms floating in this air, renders it more sensible to the eye. So that the air will appear lighter towards the horizon, and darker as well as bluer in looking up to the sky; because there is more of the thick air between our eyes and the horizon, than between our eyes and that part of the sky above our heads.

* These propositions, any more than the others mentioned in different parts of this work, were never digested into a regular treatise, as was evidently intended by the author, and consequently are not to be found, except perhaps in some of the volumes of the author's manuscript collections.

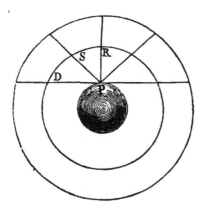

For instance : if the eye placed in P, looks through the air along the line P R, and then lowers itself a little along P S, the air will begin to appear a little whiter, because there is more of the thick air in this space than in the first. And if it be still removed lower, so as to look straight at the horizon, no more of that blue sky will be perceived which was observable along the first line P R, because there is a much greater quantity of thick air along the horizontal line P D, than along the oblique P S, or the perpendicular P R.

CHAP. CCLXXXV.—*The Cause of the Diminution of Colours.*

The natural colour of any visible object will be diminished in proportion to the density of any other substance which interposes between that object and the eye.

CHAP. CCLXXXVI.—*Of the Diminution of Colours and Objects.*

Let the colours vanish in proportion as the objects diminish in size, according to the distance.

CHAP. CCLXXXVII.—*Of the Variety observable in Colours, according to their distance or proximity.*

The local colour of such objects as are darker than the air, will appear less dark as they are more remote ; and, on the contrary, objects lighter than the air will lose their brightness in proportion to their distance from the eye. In general, all objects that are darker or lighter than the air, are discoloured by distance, which changes their quality, so that the lighter appears darker, and the darker lighter.

CHAP. CCLXXXVIII. —*At what Distance Colours are entirely lost.*

Local colours are entirely lost at a greater or less distance, according as the eye and the object are more or less elevated from the earth. This is proved by the seventh proposition*, which says

---

* See chap. ccxciii. cccvii. cccviii.

the air is more or less pure, as it is near to, or remote from the earth. If the eye, then, and the object are near the earth, the thickness of the air which interposes, will in a great measure confuse the colour of that object to the eye. But if the eye and the object are placed high above the earth, the air will disturb the natural colour of that object very little. In short, the various gradations of colour depend not only on the various distances, in which they may be lost; but also on the variety of lights, which change according to the different hours of the day, and the thickness or purity of the air, through which the colour of the object is conveyed to the eye.

CHAP. CCLXXXIX.—*Of the Change observable in the same Colour, according to its Distance from the Eye.*

Among several colours of the same nature, that which is the nearest to the eye will alter the least; because the air which interposes between the eye and the object seen, envelopes, in some measure, that object. If the air, which interposes, be in great quantity, the object seen will be strongly tinged with the colour of that air; but if the air be thin, then the view of that object, and its colour, will be very little obstructed.

CHAP. CCXC.—*Of the blueish Appearance of remote Objects in a Landscape.*

Whatever be the colour of distant objects,
the darkest, whether natural or accidental, will
appear the most tinged with azure. By the natural darkness is meant the proper colour of the
object; the accidental one is produced by the
shadow of some other body.

CHAP. CCXCI.—*Of the Qualities in the Surface
which first lose themselves by Distance.*

The first part of any colour which is lost by
the distance, is the gloss, being the smallest part
of it, as a light within a light. The second that
diminishes by being farther removed, is the light,
because it is less in quantity than the shadow.
The third is the principal shadows, nothing remaining at last but a kind of middling obscurity.

CHAP. CCXCII.—*From what cause the azure of
the Air proceeds.*

The azure of the sky is produced by the transparent body of the air, illumined by the sun, and
interposed between the darkness of the expanse
above, and the earth below. The air in itself has
no quality of smell, taste, or colour, but is easily
impregnated with the quality of other matter surrounding it; and will appear bluer in proportion

to the darkness of the space behind it, as may be
observed against the shady sides of mountains,
which are darker than any other object.   In this
instance the air appears of the most beautiful
azure, while on the other side that receives the
light, it shews through that more of the natural
colour of the mountain.

CHAP. CCXCIII.—*Of the Perspective of Colours.*

The same colour being placed at various distances and equal elevation, the force and effect of
its colouring will be according to the proportion
of the distance which there is from each of these
colours to the eye.   It is proved thus : let A B
E D be one and the same colour.   The first, E,
is placed at two degrees of distance from the eye
A; the second, B, shall be four degrees; the
third, C, six degrees; and the fourth, D, eight degrees; as appears by the circles which terminate
upon and intersect the line A R.   Let us suppose
that the space A R, S P, is one degree of thin air,
and S P E T another degree of thicker air.   It
will follow, that the first colour, E, will pass to
the eye through one degree of thick air, E S, and
through another degree, S A, of thinner air.   And
B will send its colour to the eye in A, through
two degrees of thick air, and through two others
of the thinner sort.   C will send it through three
degrees of the thin, and three of the thick sort,

I

while D goes through four degrees of the one, and four of the other. This demonstrates, that the gradation of colours is in proportion to their distance from the eye*. But this happens only to those colours which are on a level with the eye; as for those which happen to be at unequal elevations, we cannot observe the same rule, because they are in that case situated in different qualities of air, which alter and diminish these colours in various manners.

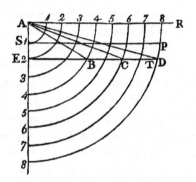

CHAP. CCXCIV.—*Of the Perspective of Colours in dark Places.*

In any place where the light diminishes in a gradual proportion, till it terminates in total darkness, the colours also will lose themselves and be dissolved in proportion as they recede from the eye.

---

* See chap. cclxxxvii.

CHAP. CCXCV.—*Of the Perspective of Colours.*

The principal colours, or those nearest to the eye, should be pure and simple; and the degree of their diminution should be in proportion to their distance, viz. the nearer they are to the principal point, the more they will possess of the purity of those colours, and they will partake of the colour of the horizon in proportion as they approach to it.

CHAP. CCXCVI.—*Of Colours.*

Of all the colours which are not blue, those that are nearest to black will, when distant, partake most of the azure; and, on the contrary, those will preserve their proper colour at the greatest distance, that are most dissimilar to black.

The green therefore of the fields will change sooner into blue than yellow, or white, which will preserve their natural colour at a greater distance than that, or even red.

CHAP. CCXCVII.—*How it happens that Colours do not change, though placed in different Qualities of Air.*

The colour will not be subject to any alteration when the distance and the quality of air have a reciprocal proportion. What it loses by the distance it regains by the purity of the air, viz. if we suppose the first or lowest air to have four degrees of

I 2

thickness, and the colour to be at one degree from the eye, and the second air above to have three degrees. The air having lost one degree of thickness, the colour will acquire one degree upon the distance. And when the air still higher shall have lost two degrees of thickness, the colour will acquire as many upon the distance; and in that case the colour will be the same at three degrees as at one. But to be brief, if the colour be raised so high as to enter that quality of air which has lost three degrees of thickness, and acquired three degrees of distance, then you may be certain that that colour which is high and remote, has lost no more than the colour which is below and nearer; because in rising it has acquired those three degrees which it was losing by the same distance from the eye; and this is what was meant to be proved.

CHAP. CXCVIII.—*Why Colours experience no apparent Change, though placed in different Qualities of Air.*

It may happen that a colour does not alter, though placed at different distances, when the thickness of the air and the distance are in the same inverse proportion. It is proved thus:—let A be the eye, and H any colour whatever, placed at one degree of distance from the eye, in a quality of air of four degrees of thickness; but be-

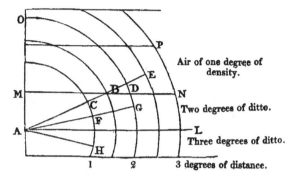

cause the second degree above, A M N L, contains a thinner air by one-half, which air conveys
this colour, it follows that this colour will appear
as if removed double the distance it was at before,
viz. at two degrees of distance, A F and F G, from
the eye; and it will be placed in G.   If that is
raised to the second degree of air A M N L, and
to the degree O M, P N, it will necessarily be
placed at E, and will be removed from the eye
the whole length of the line A E, which will be
proved in this manner to be equal in thickness to
the distance A G.   If in the same quality of air
the distance A G interposed between the eye and
the colour occupies two degrees, and A E occupies two degrees and a half, it is sufficient to preserve the colour G, when raised to E, from any
change, because the degree A C and the degree
A F being the same in thickness, are equal and
alike, and the degree C D, though equal in length

to the degree F G, is not alike in point of thickness of air; because half of it is situated in a degree of air of double the thickness of the air
above: this half degree of distance occupies as
much of the colour as one whole degree of the air
above would, which air above is twice as thin as
the air below, with which it terminates; so that
by calculating the thickness of the air, and the
distances, you will find that the colours have
changed places without undergoing any alteration
in their beauty. And we shall prove it thus:
reckoning first the thickness of the air, the colour
H is placed in four degrees of thickness, the colour G in two degrees, and E at one degree. Now
let us see whether the distances are in an equal
inverse proportion; the colour E is at two degrees
and a half of distance, G at two degrees, and H at
one degree. But as this distance has not an exact
proportion with the thickness of the air, it is necessary to make a third calculation in this manner: A C is perfectly like and equal to A F; the
half degree, C B, is like but not equal to A F, because it is only half a degree in length, which is
equal to a whole degree of the quality of the air
above; so that by this calculation we shall solve
the question. For A C is equal to two degrees
of thickness of the air above, and the half degree
C B is equal to a whole degree of the same air
above; and one degree more is to be taken in,

viz. B E, which makes the fourth.   A H has four
degrees of thickness of air, A G also four, viz.
A F two in value, and F G also two, which taken
together make four.   A E has also four, because
A C contains two, and C D one, which is the half
of A C, and in the same quality of air; and there
is a whole degree above in the thin air, which altogether make four.   So that if A E is not double
the distance A G, nor four times the distance A H,
it is made equivalent by the half degree C B of
thick air, which is equal to a whole degree of thin
air above.   This proves the truth of the proposition, that the colour H G E does not undergo any
alteration by these different distances.

CHAP. CCXCIX.—*Contrary Opinions in regard
to Objects seen afar off.*

Many painters will represent the objects darker,
in proportion as they are removed from the eye;
but this cannot be true, unless the objects seen
be white; as shall be examined in the next
chapter.

CHAP. CCC.—*Of the Colour of Objects remote
from the Eye.*

The air tinges objects with its own colour more
or less in proportion to the quantity of intervening air between it and the eye, so that a dark
object at the distance of two miles (or a density of

air equal to such distance), will be more tinged with its colour than if only one mile distant.

It is said, that, in a landscape, trees of the same species appear darker in the distance than near; this cannot be true, if they be of equal size, and divided by equal spaces. But it will be so if the first trees are scattered, and the light of the fields is seen through and between them, while the others which are farther off, are thick together, as is often the case near some river or other piece of water: in this case no space of light fields can be perceived, but the trees appear thick together, accumulating the shadow on each other. It also happens, that as the shady parts of plants are much broader than the light ones, the colour of the plants becoming darker by the multiplied shadows, is preserved, and conveyed to the eye more strongly than that of the other parts; these masses, therefore, will carry the strongest parts of their colour to a greater distance.

CHAP. CCCI.—*Of the Colour of Mountains.*

The darker the mountain is in itself, the bluer it will appear at a great distance. The highest part will be the darkest, as being more woody; because woods cover a great many shrubs, and other plants, which never receive any light. The wild plants of those woods are also naturally of a darker hue than cultivated plants; for oak, beech, fir, cypress, and pine trees are much darker than olive and other domestic plants. Near the top of these mountains, where the air is thinner and purer, the darkness of the woods will make it appear of a deeper azure, than at the bottom, where the air is thicker. A plant will detach very little from the ground it stands upon, if that ground be of a colour something similar to its own; and, *vice versâ*, that part of any white object which is nearest to a dark one, will appear the whitest, and the less so as it is removed from it; and any dark object will appear darker, the nearer it is to a white one; and less so, if removed from it.

CHAP. CCCII.—*Why the Colour and Shape of Objects are lost in some Situations apparently dark, though not so in Reality.*

There are some situations which, though light, appear dark, and in which objects are deprived both of form and colour. This is caused by the great light which pervades the intervening air; as is observable by looking in through a window at some distance from the eye, when nothing is seen but an uniform darkish shade; but if we enter the house, we shall find that room to be full of light, and soon distinguish every small object contained within that window. This difference of effect is produced by the great brightness of the air, which contracts considerably the pupil of the eye, and by so doing diminishes its power. But in dark places the pupil is enlarged, and acquires as much in strength, as it increases in size. This is proved in my second proposition of perspective.*

CHAP. CCCIII.—*Various Precepts in Painting.*

The termination and shape of the parts in general are very little seen, either in great masses of light, or of shadows; but those which are situated between the extremes of light and shade are the most distinct.

Perspective, as far as it extends in regard to painting, is divided into three principal parts; the first consists in the diminution of size according to distance; the second concerns the diminution of colours in such objects; and the third treats of the diminution of the perception altogether of those objects, and of the degree of precision they ought to exhibit at various distances.

The azure of the sky is produced by a mixture composed of light and darkness;† I say of light, because of the moist particles floating in the air, which reflect the light. By darkness, I mean the pure air, which has none of these extraneous particles to stop and reflect the rays. Of this we see an example in the air interposed between the eye

* This book on perspective was never drawn up.
† See chap. ccxcii.

and some dark mountains, rendered so by the shadows of an innumerable quantity of trees; or else shaded on one side by the natural privation of the rays of the sun; this air becomes azure, but not so on the side of the mountain which is light, particularly when it is covered with snow.

Among objects of equal darkness and equal distance, those will appear darker that terminate upon a lighter ground, and *vice versâ.**

That object which is painted with the most white and the most black, will shew greater relief than any other; for that reason I would recommend to painters to colour and dress their figures with the brightest and most lively colours; for if they are painted of a dull or obscure colour, they will detach but little, and not be much seen, when the picture is placed at some distance; because the colour of every object is obscured in the shades; and if it be represented as originally so all over, there will be but little difference between the lights and the shades, while lively colours will shew a striking difference.

* See chap. ccxii. ccxlviii. cclv.

AERIAL PERSPECTIVE.

Chap. CCCIV.—*Aerial Perspective.*

There is another kind of perspective called aerial, because by the difference of the air it is easy to determine the distance of different objects, though seen on the same line; such, for instance, as buildings behind a wall, and appearing all of the same height above it. If in your picture you want to have one appear more distant than another, you must first suppose the air somewhat thick, because, as we have said before, in such a kind of air the objects seen at a great distance, as mountains are, appear blueish like the air, by means of the great quantity of air that interposes between the eye and such mountains. You will then paint the first building behind that wall of its proper colour; the next in point of distance, less distinct in the outline, and participating, in a greater degree, of the blueish colour of the air; another, which you wish to send off as much farther, should be painted as much bluer; and if you wish one of them to appear five times farther removed beyond the wall, it must have five times more of the azure.

By this rule these buildings which appeared all of the same size, and upon the same line, will be distinctly perceived to be of different dimensions, and at different distances.

CHAP. CCCV.—*The Parts of the smallest Objects will first disappear in Painting.*

Of objects receding from the eye the smallest will be first lost to the sight; from which it follows, that the largest will be the last to disappear. The painter, therefore, ought not to finish the parts of those objects which are very far off, but follow the rule given in the sixth book.*

How many, in the representation of towns, and other objects remote from the eye, express every part of the buildings in the same manner as if they were very near. It is not so in nature, because there is no sight so powerful as to perceive distinctly at any great distance the precise form of parts or extremities of objects. The painter therefore who pronounces the outlines, and the minute distinction of parts, as several have done, will not give the representation of distant objects, but by this error will make them appear exceedingly near. Again, the angles of buildings in distant towns are not to be expressed (for they cannot be seen),

---

* There is no work of this author to which this can at present refer, but the principle is laid down in chapters cclxxiv. cccvi. of the present treatise.

considering that angles are formed by the concurrence of two lines into one point, and that a point
has no parts; it is therefore invisible.

CHAP. CCCVI.—*Small Figures ought not to be
too much finished.*

Objects appear smaller than they really are when
they are distant from the eye, and because there
is a great deal of air interposed, which weakens
the appearance of forms, and, by a natural consequence, prevents our seeing distinctly the minute
parts of such objects.   It behoves the painter
therefore to touch those parts slightly, in an unfinished manner; otherwise it would be against the
effect of Nature, whom he has chosen for his guide.
For, as we said before, objects appear small on
account of their great distance from the eye; that
distance includes a great quantity of air, which,
forming a dense body, obstructs the light, and
prevents our seeing the minute parts of the
objects.

CHAP. CCCVII.—*Why the Air is to appear whiter
as it approaches nearer to the Earth.*

As the air is thicker nearer the earth, and becomes thinner as it rises, look, when the sun is in
the east, towards the west, between the north and
south, and you will perceive that the thickest and
lowest air will receive more light from the sun

than the thinner air, because its beams meet with more resistance.

If the sky terminate low, at the end of a plain, that part of it nearest to the horizon, being seen only through the thick air, will alter and break its natural colour, and will appear whiter than over your head, where the visual ray does not pass through so much of that gross air, corrupted by earthy vapours. But if you turn towards the east, the air will be darker the nearer it approaches the earth; for the air being thicker, does not admit the light of the sun to pass so freely.

CHAP. CCCVIII.—*How to paint the distant Part of a Landscape.*

It is evident that the air is in some parts thicker and grosser than in others, particularly that nearest to the earth; and as it rises higher, it becomes thinner and more transparent. The objects which are high and large, from which you are at some distance, will be less apparent in the lower parts; because the visual ray which perceives them, passes through a long space of dense air; and it is easy to prove that the upper parts are seen by a line, which, though on the side of the eye it originates in a thick air, nevertheless, as it ascends to the highest summit of its object, terminates in an air much thinner than that of the lower parts; and for that reason the more that line or visual ray advances from the eye, it becomes, in its progress from one point to another, thinner and thinner, passing from a pure air into another which is purer; so that a painter who has mountains to represent in a landscape, ought to observe, that from one hill to another, the tops will appear always clearer than the bases. In proportion as the distance from one to another is greater, the top will be clearer; and the higher they are, the more they will show their variety of form and colour.

Chap. CCCIX.—*Of precise and confused Objects.*

The parts, that are near in the fore-ground should be finished in a bold determined manner; but those in the distance must be unfinished, and confused in their outlines.

Chap. CCCX.—*Of distant Objects.*

That part of any object which is nearest to the luminary from which it receives the light, will be the lightest.

The representation of an object in every degree of distance, loses degrees of its strength; that is, in proportion as the object is more remote from the eye it will be less perceivable through the air in its representation.

Chap. CCCXI.—*Of Buildings seen in a thick Air.*

That part of a building seen through a thick air,

will appear less distinct than another part seen through a thinner air. Therefore the eye, N,

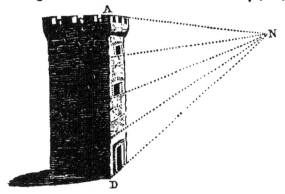

looking at the tower A D, will see it more confusedly in the lower degrees, but at the same time lighter; and as it ascends to the other degrees it will appear more distinct, but somewhat darker.

CHAP. CCCXII.—*Of Towns and other Objects seen through a thick Air.*

Buildings or towns seen through a fog, or the air made thick by smoke or other vapours, will appear less distinct the lower they are; and, *vice versâ*, they will be sharper and more visible in proportion as they are higher. We have said in chapter CCCXXI. that the air is thicker the lower it is, and thinner as it is higher. It is demonstrated also by the cut, where the tower, A F, is seen by the eye **N**, in a thick air, from **B** to **F**,

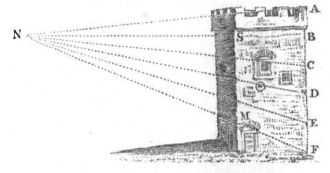

which is divided into four degrees, growing thicker
as they are nearer the bottom. The less the quantity of air interposed between the eye and its object
is, the less also will the colour of the object participate of the colour of that air. It follows, that
the greater the quantity of air interposed between
the eye and the object seen, is, the more this object will participate of the colour of the air. It is
demonstrated thus : N being the eye looking at
the five parts of the tower A F, viz. A B C D E,
I say, that if the air were of the same thickness,
there would be the same proportion between the
colour of the air at the bottom of the tower and
the colour of the air that the same tower has at
the place B, as there is in length between the line
M and F. As, however, we have supposed that
the air is not of equal thickness, but, on the contrary, thicker as it is lower, it follows, that the

proportion by which the air tinges the different elevations of the tower B C F, exceeds the proportion of the lines; because the line M F, besides its being longer than the line S B, passes by unequal degrees through a quality of air which is unequal in thickness.

CHAP. CCCXIII.—*Of the inferior Extremities of distant Objects.*

The inferior or lower extremities of distant objects are not so apparent as the upper extremities. This is observable in mountains and hills, the tops of which detach from the sides of other mountains behind. We see the tops of these more determined and distinctly than their bases; because the upper extremities are darker, being less encompassed by thick air, which always remains in the lower regions, and makes them appear dim and confused. It is the same with trees, buildings, and other objects high up. From this effect it often happens that a high tower, seen at a great distance, will appear broad at top, and narrow at bottom; because the thin air towards the top does not prevent the angles on the sides and other different parts of the tower from being seen, as the thick air does at bottom. This is demonstrated by the seventh proposition,* which says, that the thick air interposed between the eye and the sun,

* See chapters cccvii. cccxxii.

is lighter below than above, and where the air is
whiteish, it confuses the dark objects more than
if such air were blueish or thinner, as it is higher
up. The battlements of a fortress have the spaces
between equal to the breadth of the battlement,
and yet the space will appear wider; at a great
distance the battlements will appear very much
diminished, and being removed still farther, will
disappear entirely, and the fort show only the
straight wall, as if there were no battlements.

CHAP. CCCXIV.—*Which Parts of Objects disappear first by being removed farther from the Eye,
and which preserve their Appearance.*

The smallest parts are those which, by being
removed, lose their appearance first; this may be
observed in the gloss upon spherical bodies, or
columns, and the slender parts of animals; as in
a stag, the first sight of which does not discover
its legs and horns so soon as its body, which, being broader, will be perceived from a greater distance. But the parts which disappear the very
first, are the lines which describe the members,
and terminate the surface and shape of bodies.

CHAP. CCCXV.—*Why Objects are less distinguished in proportion as they are farther removed
from the Eye.*

This happens because the smallest parts are lost

first; the second, in point of size, are also lost at a somewhat greater distance, and so on successively; the parts by degrees melting away, the perception of the object is diminished; and at last all the parts, and the whole, are entirely lost to the sight.* Colours also disappear on account of the density of the air interposed between the eye and the object.

CHAP. CCCXVI.—*Why Faces appear dark at a distance.*

It is evident that the similitude of all objects placed before us, large as well as small, is perceptible to our senses through the iris of the eye. If through so small an entrance the immensity of the sky and of the earth is admitted, the faces of men (which are scarcely any thing in comparison of such large objects), being still diminished by the distance, will occupy so little of the eye, that they become almost imperceptible. Besides, having to pass through a dark medium from the surface to the *Retina* in the inside, where the impression is made, the colour of faces, (not being very strong, and rendered still more obscure by the darkness of the tube) when arrived at the focus appears dark. No other reason can be given on that point, except that the speck in the middle of the apple of the eye is black, and, being full of a transpa-

* See chap. cxvi. cxxi. cccv.

rent fluid like air, performs the same office as a hole in a board, which on looking into it appears black; and that those things which are seen through both a light and dark air, become confused and obscure.

CHAP. CCCXVII.—*Of Towns and other Buildings seen through a Fog in the Morning or Evening.*

Buildings seen afar off in the morning or in the evening, when there is a fog, or thick air, show only those parts distinctly which are enlightened by the sun towards the horizon; and the parts of those buildings which are not turned towards the sun remain confused and almost of the colour of the fog.

CHAP. CCCXVIII.—*Of the Height of Buildings seen in a Fog.*

Of a building near the eye the top parts will appear more confused than the bottom; because there is more fog between the eye and the top than at the base. And a square tower, seen at a great distance through a fog, will appear narrower at the base than at the summit. This is accounted for in chapter cccxiii. which says, that the fog will appear whiter and thicker as it approaches the ground; and, as it is said before,* that a dark object will appear smaller in proportion as it is

* See chap. cccxiii. and cccxxiii.

placed on a whiter ground. Therefore the fog`
being whiter at bottom than at top, it follows that
the tower (being darkish) will appear narrower at
the base than at the summit.

CHAP. CCCXIX.—*Why Objects which are high,
appear darker at a Distance than those which
are low, though the Fog be uniform, and of equal
Thickness.*

Amongst objects situated in a fog, thick air,
vapour, smoke, or at a distance, the highest will
be the most distinctly seen : and amongst objects
equal in height, that placed in the darkest fog, will
be most confused and dark.   As it happens to the
eye H, looking at A B C, three towers of equal

height; it sees the top C as low as R, in two degrees of thickness; and the top B, in one degree
only; therefore the top C will appear darker than
the top of the tower B.

CHAP. CCCXX.—*Of Objects seen in a Fog.*

Objects seen through a fog will appear larger than they are in reality, because the aerial perspective does not agree with the linear, viz. the colour does not agree with the magnitude of the object;* such a fog being similar to the thickness of air interposed between the eye and the horizon in fine weather. But in this case the fog is near the eye, and though the object be also near, it makes it appear as if it were as far off as the horizon; where a great tower would appear no bigger than a man placed near the eye.

* To our obtaining a correct idea of the magnitude and distance of any object seen from afar, it is necessary that we consider how much of distinctness an object loses at a distance (from the mere interposition of the air), as well as what it loses in size; and these two considerations must unite before we can decidedly pronounce as to its distance or magnitude. This calculation, as to distinctness, must be made upon the idea that the air is clear, as, if by any accident it is otherwise, we shall (knowing the proportion in which clear air dims a prospect) be led to conclude this farther off than it is, and, to justify that conclusion, shall suppose its real magnitude correspondent with the distance, at which from its degree of distinctness it appears to be. In the circumstance remarked in the text there is, however, a great deception; the fact is, that the colour and the minute parts of the object are lost in the fog, while the size of it is not diminished in proportion; and the eye being accustomed to see objects diminished in size at a great distance, supposes this to be farther off than it is, and consequently imagines it larger.

CHAP. CCCXXI.—*Of those Objects which the Eyes perceive through a Mist or thick Air.*

The nearer the air is to water, or to the ground, the thicker it becomes. It is proved by the nineteenth proposition of the second book,* that bodies rise in proportion to their weight; and it follows, that a light body will rise higher than another which is heavy.

CHAP. CCCXXII.—*Miscellaneous Observations.*

Of different objects equal in magnitude, form, shade, and distance from the eye, those will appear the smaller that are placed on the lighter ground. This is exemplified by observing the sun when seen behind a tree without leaves; all the ramifications seen against that great light are so diminished that they remain almost invisible. The same may be observed of a pole placed between the sun and the eye.

Parallel bodies placed upright, and seen through a fog, will appear larger at top than at bottom. This is proved by the ninth proposition,† which says, that a fog, or thick air, penetrated by the rays of the sun, will appear whiter the lower they are.

* This proposition, though undoubtedly intended to form a part of some future work, which never was drawn up, makes no part of the present.

† See chap. cccvii.

K

Things seen afar off will appear out of proportion, because the parts which are the lightest
will send their image with stronger rays than the
parts which are darkest. I have seen a woman
dressed in black, with a white veil over her head,
which appeared twice as large as her shoulders
covered with black.

MISCELLANEOUS OBSERVATIONS.

LANDSCAPE.

CHAP. CCCXXIII.—*Of Objects seen at a Distance.*

ANY dark object will appear lighter when removed to some distance from the eye. It follows,
by the contrary reason, that a dark object will appear still darker when brought nearer to the eye.
Therefore the inferior parts of any object whatever, placed in thick air, will appear farther from
the eye at the bottom than at the top; for that
reason the lower parts of a mountain appear farther off than its top, which is in reality the farthest.

CHAP. CCCXXIV.—*Of a Town seen through a
thick Air.*

The eye which, looking downwards, sees a town
immersed in very thick air, will perceive the top
of the buildings darker, but more distinct than the
bottom. The tops detach against a light ground,
because they are seen against the low and thick
air which is beyond them. This is a consequence
of what has been explained in the preceding
chapter.

CHAP. CCCXXV.—*How to draw a Landscape.*

Contrive that the trees in your landscape be half in shadow and half in the light. It is better to represent them as when the sun is veiled with thin clouds, because in that case the trees receive a general light from the sky, and are darkest in those parts which are nearest to the earth.

CHAP. CCCXXVI.—*Of the Green of the Country.*

Of the greens seen in the country, that of trees and other plants will appear darker than that of fields and meadows, though they may happen to be of the same quality.

CHAP. CCCXXVII.—*What Greens will appear most of a blueish Cast.*

Those greens will appear to approach nearest to blue which are of the darkest shade when remote. This is proved by the seventh proposition,* which says, that blue is composed of black and white seen at a great distance.

CHAP. CCCXXVIII.—*The Colour of the Sea from different Aspects.*

When the sea is a little ruffled it has no sameness of colour; for, whoever looks at it from the shore, will see it of a dark colour, in a greater de-

* Vide chap. ccxcii. ccciii.

gree as it approaches towards the horizon, and will perceive also certain lights moving slowly on the surface like a flock of sheep. Whoever looks at the sea from on board a ship, at a distance from the land, sees it blue. Near the shore it appears darkish, on account of the colour of the earth reflected by the water, as in a looking-glass; but at sea the azure of the air is reflected to the eye by the waves in the same manner.

CHAP. CCCXXIX.—*Why the same Prospect appears larger at some Times than at others.*

Objects in the country appear sometimes larger and sometimes smaller than they actually are, from the circumstance of the air interposed between the eye and the horizon, happening to be either thicker or thinner than usual.

Of two horizons equally distant from the eye, that which is seen through the thicker air will appear farther removed; and the other will seem nearer, being seen through a thinner air.

Objects of unequal size, but equally distant, will appear equal if the air which is between them and the eye be of proportionable inequality of thickness, viz. if the thickest air be interposed between the eye and the smallest of the objects. This is proved by the perspective of colours,* which is so deceitful that a mountain which would appear small by

* See chap. ccxcviii.

the compasses, will seem larger than a small hill near the eye; as a finger placed near the eye will cover a large mountain far off.

CHAP. CCCXXX.—*Of Smoke.*

Smoke is more transparent, though darker, towards the extremities of its waves than in the middle.

It moves in a more oblique direction in proportion to the force of the wind which impels it.

Different kinds of smoke vary in colour, as the causes that produce them are various.

Smoke never produces determined shadows, and the extremities are lost as they recede from their primary cause. Objects behind it are less apparent in proportion to the thickness of the smoke. It is whiter nearer its origin, and bluer towards its termination.

Fire appears darker, the more smoke there is interposed between it and the eye.

Where smoke is farther distant, the objects are less confused by it.

It encumbers and dims all the landscape like a fog. Smoke is seen to issue from different places, with flames at the origin, and the most dense part of it. The tops of mountains will be more seen than the lower parts, as in a fog.

CHAP. CCCXXXI. — *In what Part Smoke is lightest.*

Smoke which is seen between the sun and the eye will be lighter and more transparent than any other in the landscape. The same is observed of dust, and of fog; while, if you place yourself between the sun and those objects, they will appear dark.

CHAP. CCCXXXII.—*Of the Sun-beams passing through the Openings of Clouds.*

The sun-beams which penetrate the openings interposed between clouds of various density and form, illuminate all the places over which they pass, and tinge with their own colour all the dark places that are behind: which dark places are only seen in the intervals between the rays.

CHAP. CCCXXXIII.—*Of the Beginning of Rain.*

When the rain begins to fall, it tarnishes and darkens the air, giving it a dull colour, but receives still on one side a faint light from the sun, and is shaded on the other side, as we observe in clouds; till at last it darkens also the earth, depriving it entirely of the light of the sun. Objects seen through the rain appear confused and of undetermined shape, but those which are near will be more distinct. It is observable, that on the side where the rain is shaded, objects will be more

clearly distinguished than where it receives the
light; because on the shady side they lose only
their principal lights, whilst on the other they lose
both their lights and shadows, the lights mixing
with the light part of the rain, and the shadows
are also considerably weakened by it.

CHAP. CCCXXXIV.— *The Seasons are to be*
observed.

In Autumn you will represent the objects according as it is more or less advanced. At the
beginning of it the leaves of the oldest branches
only begin to fade, more or less, however, according as the plant is situated in a fertile or barren
country; and do not imitate those who represent
trees of every kind (though at equal distance) with
the same quality of green. Endeavour to váry
the colour of meadows, stones, trunks of trees, and
all other objects, as much as possible, for Nature
abounds in variety *ad infinitum.*

CHAP. CCCXXXV.— *The Difference of Climates*
to be observed.

Near the sea-shore, and in southern parts, you
will be careful not to represent the Winter season
by the appearance of trees and fields, as you would
do in places more inland, and in northern countries, except when these are covered with ever-
greens, which shoot afresh all the year round.

Chap. CCCXXXVI.—*Of Dust.*

Dust becomes lighter the higher it rises, and appears darker the less it is raised, when it is seen between the eye and the sun.

Chap. CCCXXXVII.—*How to represent the Wind.*

In representing the effect of the wind, besides the bending of trees, and leaves twisting the wrong side upwards, you will also express the small dust whirling upwards till it mixes in a confused manner with the air.

Chap. CCCXXXVIII.—*Of a Wilderness.*

Those trees and shrubs which are by their nature more loaded with small branches, ought to be touched smartly in the shadows, but those which have larger foliage, will cause broader shadows.

Chap. CCCXXXIX.—*Of the Horizon seen in the Water.*

By the sixth proposition,* the horizon will be seen in the water as in a looking-glass, on that side which is opposite the eye. And if the painter has to represent a spot covered with water, let him remember that the colour of it cannot be

* This was probably to have been a part of some other work, but it does not occur in this.

K 5

either lighter or darker than that of the neighbouring objects.

CHAP. CCCXL.—*Of the Shadow of Bridges on the Surface of the Water.*

The shadows of bridges can never be seen on the surface of the water, unless it should have lost its transparent and reflecting quality, and become troubled and muddy; because clear water being polished and smooth on its surface, the image of the bridge is formed in it as in a looking-glass, and reflected in all the points situated between the eye and the bridge at equal angles; and even the air is seen under the arches. These circumstances cannot happen when the water is muddy, because it does not reflect the objects any longer, but receives the shadow of the bridge in the same manner as a dusty road would receive it.

CHAP. CCCXLI.—*How a Painter ought to put in Practice the Perspective of Colours.*

To put in practice that perspective which teaches the alteration, the lessening, and even the entire loss of the very essence of colours, you must take some points in the country at the distance of about sixty-five yards* from each other; as trees, men, or some other remarkable objects. In regard to

* Cento braccia, or cubits. The Florence braccio is one foot ten inches seven-eighths, English measure.

the first tree, you will take a glass, and having fixed that well, and also your eye, draw upon it, with the greatest accuracy, the tree you see through it; then put it a little on one side, and compare it closely with the natural one, and colour it, so that in shape and colour it may resemble the original, and that by shutting one eye they may both appear painted, and at the same distance. The same rule may be applied to the second and third tree at the distance you have fixed. These studies will be very useful if managed with judgment, where they may be wanted in the offscape of a picture. I have observed that the second tree is less by four-fifths than the first, at the distance of thirteen yards.

CHAP. CCCXLII.—*Various Precepts in Painting.*

The superficies of any opake body participates of the colour of the transparent medium interposed between the eye and such body, in a greater or less degree, in proportion to the density of such medium and the space it occupies.

The outlines of opake bodies will be less apparent in proportion as those bodies are farther distant from the eye.

That part of the opake body will be the most shaded, or lightest, which is nearest to the body that shades it, or gives it light.

The surface of any opake body participates more or less of the colour of that body which gives it light, in proportion as the latter is more or less remote, or more or less strong.

Objects seen between lights and shadows will appear to have greater relievo than those which are placed wholly in the light, or wholly in shadow.

When you give strength and precision to objects seen at a great distance, they will appear as if they were very near. Endeavour that your imitation be such as to give a just idea of distances. If the object in nature appear confused in the outlines, let the same be observed in your picture.

The outlines of distant objects appear undetermined and confused, for two reasons : the first is, that they come to the eye by so small an angle, and are therefore so much diminished, that they strike the sight no more than small objects do, which though near can hardly be distinguished, such as the nails of the fingers, insects, and other similar things : the second is, that between the eye and the distant objects there is so much air interposed, that it becomes thick; and, like a veil, tinges the shadows with its own whiteness, and turns them from a dark colour to another between black and white, such as azure.

Although, by reason of the great distance, the appearance of many things is lost, yet those things which receive the light from the sun will be more discernible, while the rest remain enveloped in confused shadows.   And because the air is thicker near the ground, the things which are lower will appear confused; and *vice versâ*.

When the sun tinges the clouds on the horizon with red, those objects which, on account of their distance, appear blueish, will participate of that redness, and will produce a mixture between the azure and red, which renders the prospect lively and pleasant; all the opake bodies which receive that light will appear distinct, and of a reddish colour, and the air, being transparent, will be impregnated with it, and appear of the colour of *lilies*.*

The air which is between the earth and the sun when it rises or sets, will always dim the objects it surrounds, more than the air any where else, because it is whiter.

It is not necessary to mark strongly the outlines of any object which is placed upon another.   It ought to detach of itself.

If the outline or extremity of a white and curved surface terminate upon another white body, it will have a shade at that extremity, darker than any part of the light; but if against a dark object, such outline, or extremity, will be lighter than any part of the light.

Those objects which are most different in colour, will appear the most detached from each other.

* Probably the Author here means yellow lilies, or fleurs de lis.

Those parts of objects which first disappear in the distance, are extremities similar in colour, and ending one upon the other, as the extremities of an oak tree upon another oak similar to it. The next to disappear at a greater distance are, objects of mixed colours, when they terminate one upon the other, as trees, ploughed fields, walls, heaps of rubbish, or of stones. The last extremities of bodies that vanish are those which, being light, terminate upon a dark ground; or being dark, upon a light ground.

Of objects situated above the eye, at equal heights, the farthest removed from the eye will appear the lowest; and if situated below the eye, the nearest to it will appear the lowest. The parallel lines situated sidewise will concur to one point.*

Those objects which are near a river, or a lake, in the distant part of a landscape, are less apparent and distinct than those that are remote from them.

Of bodies of equal density, those that are nearest to the eye will appear thinnest, and the most remote thickest.

A large eye-ball will see objects larger than a small one. The experiment may be made by looking at any of the celestial bodies, through a pin-

* That point is always found in the horizon, and is called the point of sight, or the vanishing point.

hole, which being capable of admitting but a portion of its light, it seems to diminish and lose of its size in the same proportion as the pin-hole is smaller than the usual apparent size of the object.

A thick air interposed between the eye and any object, will render the outlines of such object undetermined and confused, and make it appear of a larger size than it is in reality; because the linear perspective does not diminish the angle which conveys the object to the eye. The aerial perspective carries it farther off, so that the one removes it from the eye, while the other preserves its magnitude.*

When the sun is in the West the vapours of the earth fall down again and thicken the air, so that objects not enlightened by the sun remain dark and confused, but those which receive its light will be tinged yellow and red, according to the sun's appearance on the horizon. Again, those that receive its light are very distinct, particularly public buildings and towns in houses and villages, because their shadows are dark, and it seems as if those parts which are plainly seen were coming out of confused and undetermined foundations, because at that time every thing is of one and the same colour, except what is enlightened by the sun.†

Any object receiving the light from the sun,

* See chap. cccxx.　　　　† See chap. cccxvii.

receives also the general light; so that two kinds
of shadows are produced: the darkest of the two
is that which happens to have its central line directed towards the centre of the sun.   The central
lines of the primitive and secondary lights are the
same as the central lines of the primitive and secondary shadows.

The setting sun is a beautiful and magnificent
object when it tinges with its colour all the great
buildings of towns, villages, and the top of high
trees in the country.   All below is confused and
almost lost in a tender and general mass; for, being only enlightened by the air, the difference between the shadows and the lights is small, and for
that reason it is not much detached.   But those
that are high are touched by the rays of the sun,
and, as was said before, are tinged with its colour;
the painter therefore ought to take the same colour with which he has painted the sun, and employ it in all those parts of his work which receive
its light.

It also happens very often, that a cloud will appear dark without receiving any shadow from a
separate cloud, according to the situation of the
eye; because it will see only the shady part of the
one, while it sees both the enlightened and shady
parts of the other.

Of two objects at equal height, that which is the
farthest off will appear the lowest.   Observe the

first cloud in the cut, though it is lower than the second, it appears as if it were higher. This is demonstrated by the section of the pyramidical rays of the low cloud at M A, and the second

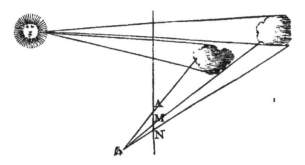

(which is higher) at N M, below M A. This happens also when, on account of the rays of the setting or rising sun, a dark cloud appears higher than another which is light.

Chap. CCCXLIII.—*The Brilliancy of a Landscape.*

The vivacity and brightness of colours in a landscape will never bear any comparison with a landscape in nature when illumined by the sun, unless the picture be placed so as to receive the same light from the sun itself.

MISCELLANEOUS OBSERVATIONS.

CHAP. CCCXLIV.—*Why a painted Object does not appear so far distant as a real one, though they be conveyed to the Eye by equal Angles.*

IF a house be painted on the pannel B C, at the

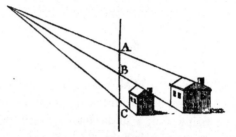

apparent distance of one mile, and by the side of it a real one be perceived at the true distance of one mile also; which objects are so disposed, that the pannel, or picture, A C, intersects the pyramidical rays with the same opening of angles; yet these two objects will never appear of the same size, nor at the same distance, if seen with both eyes.*

* This position has been already laid down in chapter cxxiv. (and will also be found in chapter cccxlviii.); and the reader is referred to the note on that passage, which will also explain that in the text, for further illustration. It may, however, be proper to re-

CHAP. CCCXLV.—*How to draw a Figure standing upon its Feet, to appear forty Braccia* * *high, in a Space of twenty Braccia, with proportionate Members.*

In this, as in any other case, the painter is not to mind what kind of surface he has to work upon; particularly if his painting is to be seen from a determined point, such as a window, or any other opening. Because the eye is not to attend to the evenness or roughness of the wall, but only to

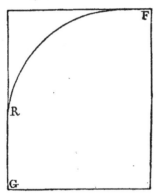

mark, that though the author has here supposed both objects conveyed to the eye by an angle of the same extent, they cannot, in fact, be so seen, unless one eye be shut; and the reason is this : if viewed with both eyes, there will be two points of sight, one in the centre of each eye; and the rays from each of these to the objects must of course be different, and will consequently form different angles.

* The braccio is one foot ten inches and seven-eighths English measure,

what is to be represented as beyond that wall; such as a landscape, or any thing else. Nevertheless a curved surface, such as F R G, would be the best, because it has no angles.

CHAP. CCCXLVI.—*How to draw a Figure twenty-four Braccia high, upon a Wall twelve Braccia high.* Plate XXII.

Draw upon part of the wall M N, half the figure you mean to represent; and the other half upon the cove above, M R. But before that, it will be necessary to draw upon a flat board, or a paper, the profile of the wall and cove, of the same shape and dimension, as that upon which you are to paint. Then draw also the profile of your figure, of whatever size you please, by the side of it; draw all the lines to the point F, and where they intersect the profile M R, you will have the dimensions of your figure as they ought to be drawn upon the real spot. You will find, that on the straight part of the wall M N, it will come of its proper form, because the going off perpendicularly will diminish it naturally; but that part which comes upon the curve will be diminished upon your drawing. The whole must be traced afterwards upon the real spot, which is similar to M N. This is a good and safe method.

CHAP. CCCXLVII.—*Why, on measuring a Face, and then painting it of the same Size, it will appear larger than the natural one.*

A B is the breadth of the space, or of the head, and it is placed on the paper at the distance C F, where the cheeks are, and it would have to stand back all A C, and then the temples would be carried to the distance O R of the lines A F, B F; so that there is the difference C O and R D.   It follows that the line C F, and the line D F, in order to become shorter,* have to go and find the paper where the whole height is drawn, that is to say, the lines F A, and F B, where the true size is; and so it makes the difference, as I have said, of C O, and R D.

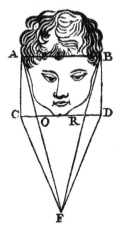

* i. e. To be abridged according to the rules of perspective.

CHAP. CCCXLVIII.—*Why the most perfect Imitation of Nature will not appear to have the same Relief as Nature itself.*

If nature is seen with two eyes, it will be impossible to imitate it upon a picture so as to appear with the same relief, though the lines, the lights, shades, and colour, be perfectly imitated.* It is proved thus: let the eyes A B, look at the object C, with the concurrence of both the central visual rays A C and B C. I say, that the sides of the visual angles (which contain these central rays) will see the space G D, behind the object C. The eye A will see all the space F D, and the eye B all the space G E. Therefore the two eyes will see behind the object C all the space F E; for which

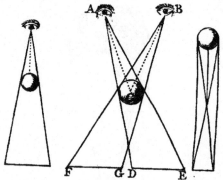

reason that object C becomes as it were transparent, according to the definition of transparent

* See chap. cxxii.

bodies, behind which nothing is hidden. This cannot happen if an object were seen with one eye only, provided it be larger than the eye. From all that has been said, we may conclude, that a painted object, occupying all the space it has behind, leaves no possible way to see any part of the ground, which it covers entirely by its own circumference.*

CHAP. CCCXLIX.—*Universality of Painting; a Precept.*

A painter cannot be said to aim at universality in the art, unless he love equally every species of that art. For instance, if he delight only in landcape, his can be esteemed only as a simple investigation; and, as our friend Botticello† remarks,

---

* The whole of this chapter, like the next but one preceding, depends on the circumstance of there being in fact two points of sight, one in the centre of each eye, when an object is viewed with both eyes. In natural objects the effect which this circumstance produces is, that the rays from each point of sight, diverging as they extend towards the object, take in not only that, but some part also of the distance behind it, till at length, at a certain distance behind it, they cross each other; whereas, in a painted representation, there being no real distance behind the object, but the whole being a flat surface, it is impossible that the rays from the points of sight should pass beyond that flat surface; and as the object itself is on that flat surface, which is the real extremity of the view, the eyes cannot acquire a sight of any thing beyond.

† A well-known painter at Florence, contemporary with Leonardo da Vinci, who painted several altar-pieces and other public works.

is but a vain study; since, by throwing a sponge impregnated with various colours against a wall, it leaves some spots upon it, which may appear like a landscape. It is true also, that a variety of compositions may be seen in such spots, according to the disposition of mind with which they are considered; such as heads of men, various animals, battles, rocky scenes, seas, clouds, woods, and the like. It may be compared to the sound of bells, which may seem to say whatever we choose to imagine. In the same manner also, those spots may furnish hints for compositions, though they do not teach us how to finish any particular part; and the imitators of them are but sorry landscape-painters.

CHAP. CCCL.—*In what Manner the Mirror is the true Master of Painters.*

When you wish to know if your picture be like the object you mean to represent, have a flat looking-glass, and place it so as to reflect the object you have imitated, and compare carefully the original with the copy. You see upon a flat mirror the representation of things which appear real; Painting is the same. They are both an even superficies, and both give the idea of something beyond their superficies. Since you are persuaded that the looking-glass, by means of lines and shades, gives you the representation of things as if they were real; you being in possession of co-

lours which in their different lights and shades are
stronger than those of the looking-glass, may certainly, if you employ the rules with judgment, give
to your picture the same appearance of Nature as
you admire in the looking-glass.   Or rather, your
picture will be like Nature itself seen in a large
looking-glass.

This looking-glass (being your master) will show
you the lights and shades of any object whatever.
Amongst your colours there are some lighter than
the lightest part of your model, and also some
darker than the strongest shades; from which it
follows, that you ought to represent Nature as
seen in your looking-glass, when you look at it
with one eye only; because both eyes surround
the objects too much, particularly when they are
small.*

CHAP. CCCLI.—*Which Painting is to be esteemed
the best.*

That painting is the most commendable which
has the greatest conformity to what is meant to be
imitated. This kind of comparison will often put
to shame a certain description of painters, who
pretend they can mend the works of Nature; as
they do, for instance, when they pretend to represent a child twelve months old, giving him eight
heads in height, when Nature in its best propor-

* See chapters ccxxiv. and cccxlviii.

L

tion admits but five. The breadth of the shoulders
also, which is equal to the head, they make double,
giving to a child a year old, the proportions of a
man of thirty. They have so often practised, and
seen others practise these errors, that they have
converted them into habit, which has taken so
deep root in their corrupted judgment, that they
persuade themselves that Nature and her imitators
are wrong in not following their own practice.*

CHAP. CCCLII.—*Of the Judgment to be made of
a Painter's Work.*

The first thing to be considered is, whether the
figures have their proper relief, according to their
respective situations, and the light they are in:
that the shadows be not the same at the extremities of the groups, as in the middle; because being surrounded by shadows, or shaded only on one
side, produce very different effects. The groups
in the middle are surrounded by shadows from the
other figures, which are between them and the
light. Those which are at the extremities have
the shadows only on one side, and receive the light
on the other. The strongest and smartest touches
of shadows are to be in the interstice between the
figures of the principal group where the light cannot penetrate.†

Secondly, that by the order and disposition of

* See chap. x.　　　† See chap. cci.

the figures they appear to be accommodated to the subject, and the true representation of the history in question.

Thirdly, that the figures appear alive to the occasion which brought them together, with expressions suited to their attitudes.

CHAP. CCCLIII.—*How to make an imaginary Animal appear natural.*

It is evident that it will be impossible to invent any animal without giving it members, and these members must individually resemble those of some known animal.

If you wish, therefore, to make a chimera, or imaginary animal, appear natural (let us suppose a serpent); take the head of a mastiff, the eyes of a cat, the ears of a porcupine, the mouth of a hare, the brows of a lion, the temples of an old cock, and the neck of a sea tortoise.*

CHAP. CCCLIV.—*Painters are not to imitate one another.*

One painter ought never to imitate the manner of any other; because in that case he cannot be called the child of Nature, but the grandchild. It is always best to have recourse to Nature, which

* Leonardo da Vinci was remarkably fond of this kind of inventions, and is accused of having lost a great deal of time that way.

is replete with such abundance of objects, than to the productions of other masters, who learnt every thing from her.

CHAP. CCCLV.—*How to judge of one's own Work.*

It is an acknowledged fact, that we perceive errors in the works of others more readily than in our own. A painter, therefore, ought to be well instructed in perspective, and acquire a perfect knowledge of the dimensions of the human body; he should also be a good architect, at least as far as concerns the outward shape of buildings, with their different parts; and where he is deficient, he ought not to neglect taking drawings from Nature.

It will be well also to have a looking-glass by him, when he paints, to look often at his work in it, which being seen the contrary way, will appear as the work of another hand, and will better shew his faults. It will be useful also to quit his work often, and take some relaxation, that his judgment may be clearer at his return; for too great application and sitting still is sometimes the cause of many gross errors.

CHAP. CCCLVI.—*Of correcting Errors which you discover.*

Remember, that when, by the exercise of your

own judgment, or the observation of others, you discover any errors in your work, you immediately set about correcting them, lest, in exposing your works to the public, you expose your defects also. Admit not any self-excuse, by persuading yourself that you shall retrieve your character, and that by some succeeding work you shall make amends for your shameful negligence; for your work does not perish as soon as it is out of your hands, like the sound of music, but remains a standing monument of your ignorance. If you excuse yourself by saying that you have not time for the study necessary to form a great painter, having to struggle against necessity, you yourself are only to blame; for the study of what is excellent is food both for mind and body. How many philosophers, born to great riches, have given them away, that they might not be retarded in their pursuits!

CHAP. CCCLVII.—*The best Place for looking at a Picture.*

Let us suppose, that A B is the picture, receiving the light from D; I say, that whoever is placed between C and E will see the picture very badly, particularly if it be painted in oil, or varnished; because it will shine, and will appear almost of the nature of a looking-glass. For these reasons, the nearer you go towards C, the less you will be able to see, because of the light from the window upon the picture, sending its reflection to that point. But if you place yourself between E D, you may conveniently see the picture, and the more so as you draw nearer to the point D, because that place is less liable to be struck by the reflected rays.

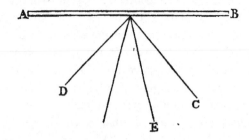

Chap. CCCLVIII.—*Of Judgment.*

There is nothing more apt to deceive us than our own judgment, in deciding on our own works; and we should derive more advantage from having our faults pointed out by our enemies, than by hearing the opinions of our friends, because they are too much like ourselves, and may deceive us as much as our own judgment.

Chap. CCCLIX.—*Of Employment anxiously wished for by Painters.*

And you, painter, who are desirous of great

practice, understand, that if you do not rest it on
the good foundation of Nature, you will labour
with little honour and less profit; and if you do it
on a good ground, your works will be many and
good, to your great honour and advantage.

CHAP. CCCLX.—*Advice to Painters.*

A painter ought to study universal Nature, and
reason much within himself on all he sees, making
use of the most excellent parts that compose the
species of every object before him. His mind will
by this method be like a mirror, reflecting truly
every object placed before it, and become, as it
were, a second Nature.

CHAP. CCCLXI.—*Of Statuary.*

To execute a figure in marble, you must first
make a model of it in clay, or plaster, and when
it is finished, place it in a square case, equally ca
pable of receiving the block of marble intended to
be shaped like it. Have some peg-like sticks to
pass through holes made in the sides, and all
round the case; push them in till every one
touches the model, marking what remains of the
sticks outwards with ink, and making a counter-
mark to every stick and its hole, so that you may
at pleasure replace them again. Then having
taken out the model, and placed the block of marble in its stead, take so much out of it, till all the

pegs go in at the same holes to the marks you had
made.   To facilitate the work, contrive your frame
so that every part of it, separately, or all together,
may be lifted up, except the bottom, which must
remain under the marble.   By this method you
may chop it off with great facility*.

CHAP. CCCLXII.—*On the Measurement and Division of Statues into Parts.*

Divide the head into twelve parts, each part into twelve degrees, each degree into twelve minutes, and these minutes into seconds†.

CHAP. CCCLXIII.—*A Precept for the Painter.*

The painter who entertains no doubt of his own
ability, will attain very little.   When the work
succeeds beyond the judgment, the artist acquires
nothing; but when the judgment is superior to
the work, he never ceases improving, if the love
of gain do not retard his progress.

* The method here recommended, was the general and common practice at that time, and continued so with little, if any
variation, till lately.   But about thirty years ago, the late Mr.
Bacon invented an entirely new method, which, as better answer-
ing the purpose, he constantly used, and from him others have
also adopted it into practice.

† This may be a good method of dividing the figure for the
purpose of reducing from large to small, or *vice versâ;* but it not
being the method generally used by the painters for measuring
their figures, as being too minute, this chapter was not introduced
amongst those of general proportions.

CHAP. CCCLXIV.—*On the Judgment of Painters.*

When the work is equal to the knowledge and judgment of the painter, it is a bad sign; and when it surpasses the judgment, it is still worse, as is the case with those who wonder at having succeeded so well. But when the judgment surpasses the work, it is a perfectly good sign; and the young painter who possesses that rare disposition, will, no doubt, arrive at great perfection. He will produce few works, but they will be such as to fix the admiration of every beholder.

CHAP. CCCLXV.—*That a Man ought not to trust to himself, but ought to consult Nature.*

Whoever flatters himself that he can retain in his memory all the effects of Nature, is deceived, for our memory is not so capacious; therefore consult Nature for every thing.

TABLE OF CHAPTERS.

The Number at the End of each Title refers to the corres-
ponding Chapter in the original Edition in Italian.

DRAWING.

PROPORTION.

MOTION AND EQUIPOISE OF FIGURES.

INVENTION OR COMPOSITION.

LIGHT AND SHADOW,

COLOURS and COLOURING.

COLOURS.

CHAP.

COLOURS IN REGARD TO LIGHT AND SHADOW.

M

CHAP.

MISCELLANEOUS OBSERVATIONS.

LANDSCAPE.

THE END.

J. B. Nichols and Son, 25, Parliament-street.

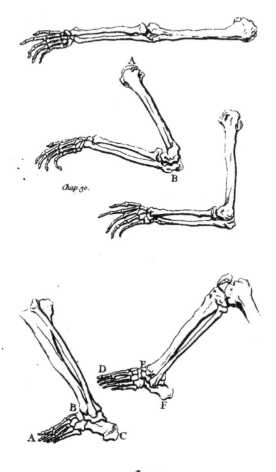

Chap. 30.

Chap. 31

Published by Nichols & Son. Parliament Street, 1836.

Printed from Stone by Standidge & C? London.

Plate 2.

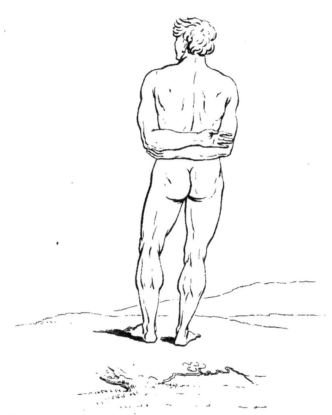

Plate 3.

Chap. 54.

Published by Nichols & Son Parliament Street, 1835.

Printed in colours by Stanandye & Co. London

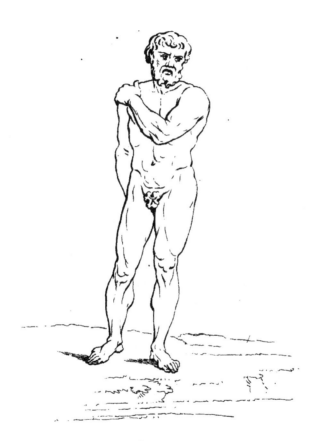

Chap. 58.

Published by Nichols & Son, Parliament Street 1835

Printed from zinc by Standidge & C° London

Plate 5.

Chap. 62.

Published by Nichols & Son, Parliament Street 1835.

Printed from Stone by Standidge & C.º London

6.

Chap. 66.

Published by Nichols & Son, Parliament Street, 1835.

Printed from Stone by Standidge & Co. London.

Plate 7.

Chap. 67.

Published by Nichols & Son, Parliament Street, 1835.

Printed from Stone by Standidge & Cᵒ London.

Pl. 8.

Chap. 71.

Published by Nichols & Son, Parliament Street, 1835.

Printed from Stone by Standidge & C.º London.

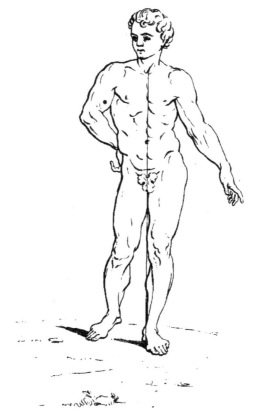

Plate 9.

Chap. 78.

Published by Nichols & Son, Parliament Street, 1835.

Printed from Stone by Standidge & C.° London.

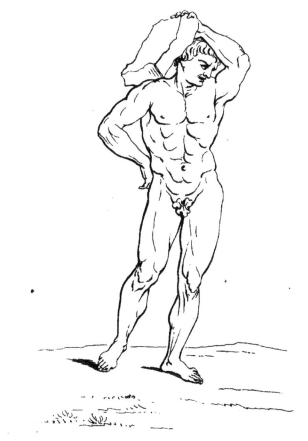

Plate 20.

Chap. 8o.

Published by Nichols & Son, Parliament Street, 1835.

Printed from Stone by Standidge & Cº. London.

B

Plate 11.

Chap. 84.

Published by Nichols & Son, Parliament Street, 1835.

Printed from Stone by Standridge & C? London.

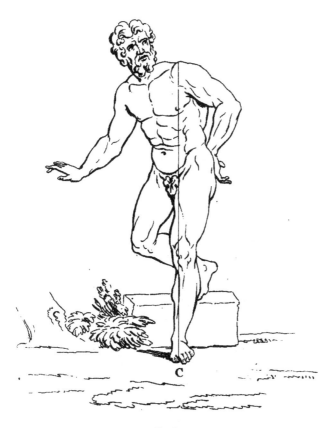

C

Chap. 84.

Published by Nichols & Son. Parliament Street. 1835.

Printed from Stone by Standidge & C° London.

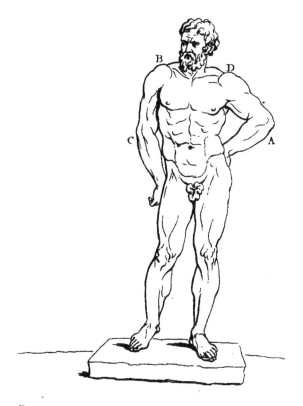

Plate 13.

Chap. 85.

Published by Nichols & Son, Parliament Street, 1835.

Printed from Stone by Standidge & C° London

Pte 14.

Chap. 89.

Published by Nichols & Son, Parliament Street, 1835.

Printed from Stone by Standidge & Cº London.

Plate 15.

Chap. 90.

Published by Nichols & Son, Parliament Street, 1835.

Printed from Stone by Standidge & Cº. London.

E

B

A

uc 16.

Chap. 92.

Published by Nichols & Son. Parliament Street. 1835.

Printed from Stone by Standidge & Cº London.

Chap. 90.

Published by Nichols & Son, Parliament Street, 1835.

Printed from Stone by Standidge & C.º London.

Plate 16.

Chap. 145.

Published by Nichols & Son, Parliament Street, 1835.

Printed from Stone by Standidge & C° London

Plate 29.

Chap. 147.

Published by Nichols & Son. Parliament Street, 1835.

Printed from Stone by Standidge & Co. London.

Published by Nichols & Son, Parliament Street, 1835.

Printed from Stone by Standidge & C.º, London.

Plate 20.

Chap. 453.

A

B

Published by Nichols & Son, Parliament Street, 1835.

Printed from Stone by Standidge & Co. London.

Plate 21.

Chap. 453.

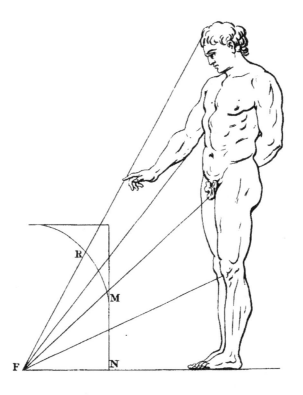

R

M

F N

Chap. 346.

Published by Nichols & Son, Parliament Street. 1835.

Printed from Stone by Standidge & C⁰ London.

CPSIA information can be obtained at www.ICGtesting.com
Printed in the USA
BVOW06*2154210116

433843BV00005B/19/P

9 781298 835956